Preface

Today, awareness has increased. The liberalization and globalization has bought significant and broad-based. So, the students should acquire the conceptual thought towards interview scenario. The book provides update material on relate with financial aspects like accounting financial terms, capital market and derivative terms, abbreviation, etc., with some interview tips, which helps in better understanding for the finance specialization students, basically MFC, MBA (Finance), PGDM, BBA, B.Com. students. This book, also helpful to the students towards interview practices. I am sure the readers will find it very useful and develop curiosity as they scan through the different terms.

I am particularly grateful to my parents who have always been a source of inspiration to me. I am grateful to Mr. Niraj Pandeyjee of M/s Himalaya Publishing House who have given me the opportunity in bringing out this book. I am deeply thankful to Mr. B.K Ojha, who always encouraged me in completing this venture.

My special thanks to all those who helped me in one way or the other, encouraged me to continue this task.

Dr. K. R. Swain

Financial Terms at a Glance

By

Dr. Kirti Ranjan Swain
Asst. Professor., IRSAR,
Cuttack, ODISHA.

First Edition : 2011

Himalaya Publishing House

MUMBAI • NEW DELHI • NAGPUR • BENGALURU • HYDERABAD • CHENNAI • PUNE • LUCKNOW • AHMEDABAD • ERNAKULAM • BHUBANESWAR • INDORE • KOLKATA • GUWAHATI

First Edition : 2011

Published by	:	Mrs. Meena Pandey for **Himalaya Publishing House Pvt. Ltd.**, "Ramdoot", Dr. Bhalerao Marg, Girgaon, **Mumbai - 400 004.** Phone: 022-23860170/23863863, Fax: 022-23877178 **E-mail: himpub@vsnl.com; Website: www.himpub.com**
Branch Offices	:	
New Delhi	:	"Pooja Apartments", 4-B, Murari Lal Street, Ansari Road, Darya Ganj, New Delhi - 110 002. Phone: 011-23270392, 23278631; Fax: 011-23256286
Nagpur	:	Kundanlal Chandak Industrial Estate, Ghat Road, Nagpur - 440 018. Phone: 0712-2738731, 3296733; Telefax: 0712-2721215
Bengaluru	:	No. 16/1 (Old 12/1), 1st Floor, Next to Hotel Highlands, Madhava Nagar, Race Course Road, Bengaluru - 560 001. Phone: 080-32919385; Telefax: 080-22286611
Hyderabad	:	No. 3-4-184, Lingampally, Besides Raghavendra Swamy Matham, Kachiguda, Hyderabad - 500 027. Phone: 040-27560041, 27550139; Mobile: 09848130433
Chennai	:	No. 85/50, Bazullah Road, T. Nagar, Chennai - 600 017. Phone: 044-28144004/28144005
Pune	:	First Floor, "Laksha" Apartment, No. 527, Mehunpura, Shaniwarpeth (Near Prabhat Theatre), Pune - 411 030. Phone: 020-24496323/24496333
Lucknow	:	Jai Baba Bhavan, Church Road, Near Manas Complex and Dr. Awasthi Clinic, Aliganj, Lucknow - 226 024. Phone: 0522-2339329, 4068914; Mobile: 09305302158, 09415349385, 09389593752
Ahmedabad	:	114, "SHAIL", 1st Floor, Opp. Madhu Sudan House, C.G. Road, Navrang Pura, Ahmedabad - 380 009. Phone: 079-26560126; Mobile: 09327324149, 09377088847
Ernakulam	:	39/104 A, Lakshmi Apartment, Karikkamuri Cross Rd., Ernakulam, Cochin - 622011, Kerala. Phone: 0484-2378012, 2378016; Mobile: 09344199799
Bhubaneswar	:	5 Station Square, Bhubaneswar - 751 001 (Odisha). Phone: 0674-2532129, Mobile: 09861046007
Indore	:	Kesardeep Avenue Extension, 73, Narayan Bagh, Flat No. 302, IIIrd Floor, Near Humpty Dumpty School, Indore - 452 007 (M.P.). Mobile: 09301386468
Kolkata	:	108/4, Beliaghata Main Road, Near ID Hospital, Opp. SBI Bank, Kolkata - 700 010, Phone: 033-32449649, Mobile: 09910440956
Guwahati	:	House No. 15, Behind Pragjyotish College, Near Sharma Printing Press, P.O. Bharalumukh, Guwahati - 781009, (Assam). Mobile: 09883055590, 09883055536
DTP by	:	HPH, Editorial Office, Bhandup (Anupama. K)
Printed at	:	**7 Hills Offset Printers,** Hyderabad.

Contents

1 Glossary: Financial Term

A

Abnormal Losses: The loss which is arising due to the negligence in the production process. By the nature, it should have been avoided if certain precautions are taken.

Absorption Costing: It is a method of allocating all indirect manufacturing costs to products.

Account: It is a part of double entry records, containing details of business transactions for a specific format.

Accounting: It is a process of identifying, classifying, recording, measuring and communicating economic information to the user group for the necessary information.

Accounting Cycle: The sequence in which data is recorded and processed until it becomes part of the financial statements at the end of the period.

Accounting Equation: Accounting equation is treated as the heart of double-entry bookkeeping. It simply stated that

Capital = Assets – Liabilities or Assets = Capital/Source of Funds — Liabilities

Accounting Information System (AIS): AIS comprises of all the inputs, storage, transaction processing, collating, and reporting of financial transacticn data.

Accounting Periods: The period of time used by the business to process its accounts and to produce reports relate with the Profit and Loss Accounts and the balance sheet. It generally starting from 1st April to 31st March every year.

Accounting Policies: Accounting policies involves principles, rules and practices applied by an entity that specify how the effects of transactions and other events are to be reflected in its financial statements.

Accounts Receivable: An accounts receivable is the *nominal* ledger which contains the overall balance of the sales ledger.

Accretive: The term accretive generally arise at the time of when one company acquires another company. And the deal is called as 'accretive to earnings'; it means that the resulting *P/E ratio* (price/earnings) of the acquired company is less than the acquiring company.

Accrual Accounting: An accounting method that tries to match the recognition of revenues earned with the expenses incurred. With the accrual method, income and expenses are recorded as they occur. An example is a sale on credit.

Accruals: The accruals process allows a business to adjust the monthly accounts for payments made in arrears. There are certain expenses that are paid for sometime after they have been used. For example, electricity charges. In simple the term accruals means outstanding.

Accrued Expense: It is an expense for which the benefit has been received, but has not been paid for by the end of the period. It generally shown in the balance sheet under current liabilities as 'accruals'.

Accrued Income: Accrued income is normally from a source of income of business. Such as rent receivable on an unused office in the company headquarters, that was due to be received by the end of the period, but which has not been received by that date. It is added to debtors in the balance sheet.

Accumulated Depreciation Account (ADA): This account is used to accumulate depreciation for balance sheet purposes and used to leave the cost or valuation figure as the balance in the fixed asset account.

Accumulated Fund: Accumulated fund is a form of capital account for a non-profit-oriented organization.

Acid Test Ratio: ATR is the ratio to find out whether the business has sufficient liquid resources to meet its current liabilities or not. It calculated are:

Acid Test Ratio = (Current Assets - Stock) ÷ Current Liabilities

It probably the most important one of all and an attempt to indicate how easily a company could pay its debts without selling its stock.

Activity-based Costing: Activity-based costing is the process of using cost drivers as the basis for overhead absorption.

Active Management: An active fund manager is one who tries to outperform stock market indices by skilfully selecting winning stocks.

Advisory Stockbroker: An advisory stockbroker is a broker who gives personalized advice on what shares or other investments to purchase or sell.

Adverse Variance: A difference arising that is apparently 'bad' from the perspective of the organization. For example, when the total actual materials cost exceeds the total standard cost due to more materials having been used than anticipated.

Aged Debtors: Aged debtors are the debtors who have owed money to the business for a defined period of time.

Allocation: It is the process by which payments are matched against purchase invoices, and receipts against sales invoices raised.

Alternative Investment Market (AIM)

It is designed as a separate market for the shares of smaller growing companies that are not yet ready for a full listing on the London Stock Exchange. It allows them access to investment capital without the cost and regulatory burdens of a full listing on the main market. It is usually used as a stepping stone to the main market.

Amortization: The process of writing off an intangible asset is called as amortization. In accounting, amortization refers to expensing the acquisition cost minus the residual value of intangible assets in a systematic manner.

Analyzed Sales Day Book: A sales day book where the net figures are analyzed into the different type of sales.

Annuity: An income-generating investment whereby, in return for the payment of a single lump sum, the annuitant receives regular amounts of income over a predefined period.

Annual Management Charge (AMC)

It is a charge paid to a company for managing your investments. The charge can vary from 0.5 per cent to around 1.5 per cent, and is dependent upon the type of investment and the degree of advice received.

Annual General Meeting (AGM)

It is the annual shareholders meeting of the companies. All companies apart from the very small are required to have an annual general meeting by law.

Annual Percentage Rate (APR)

The APR is the interest rate figure that indicates the total cost of borrowing, including any charges. When you borrow money, every lender is required by law to quote this rate. It was introduced as part of the Consumer Credit Act of 1974 and it is mostly used for credit cards, personal loans and mortgages.

Approved Investment Trust Company (AITC)

An investment trust company that doesn't have to pay capital gains tax on profits, that it makes from the sale of investments within its portfolio.

Appropriation Account: Appropriation account show the way that net profit is distributed usually in the form of cash dividend between partnership business or between the shareholders and reserve funds in a company.

Arbitration: In arbitration an independent third party considers both sides in a dispute, and makes a decision to resolve it. The arbitrator is impartial; this means he or she does not take sides. In most cases the arbitrator's decision is legally binding on both sides, so it is not possible to go to court if you are unhappy with the decision.

Arbitrage: It is a process of buying securities at a low price in one market and simultaneously selling them in another market at a higher price to make a profit. In share trading, investors called risk arbitrageurs attempt to make profits from an expected rise in the price of a takeover target's shares and a drop in the price of the bidding company's shares.

Assets: An asset is something that is of value to a company. It may be tangible and intangible assets. Tangible assets include property, vehicles, stock, cash, money held in the bank and debtors, etc. It further categorized into Fixed Assets and Current Assets. But the intangible assets include patents, copyrights, trademarks and goodwill.

Associates: The term associates include family members, relatives, partners and their relatives, employees, employers, trustees in certain trust relationships, and companies which the individual controls. Associates of companies include other companies under common control.

Ask Price: The ask price is the lowest price at which an investment can be sold at a given moment.

Association of Investment Trust Companies (AITC): The AITC is the main trade body representing over 300 investment trusts. The industry has often laboured in the shadow of unit trusts, even though investment trusts are generally cheaper and can offer better returns over the long-term.

Association of Unit Trusts and Investment Funds (AUTIF): AUTIF is the main trade association for the retail fund management industry. It promotes investment in mutual funds, such as Unit Trusts and Open Ended Investment Companies (OEICs), including Individual Savings Accounts (ISAs) and Personal Equity Plans (PEPs).

Auditor: An auditor is a person who qualified to inspect, correct and verify business accounts.

Audit Trail: A register of the details of all accounting transactions and dealt with from start to finish.

Authorized or Licensed Insolvency Practitioner: The person usually an accountant or solicitor authorized by the Department of Trade and Industry (DTI) or a recognized professional body to act as trustee, nominee, supervisor, liquidator, administrative receiver or administrator.

Authorized Share Capital: The total value of shares that the company could issue, as distinct from the up and paid-up share capital.

B

Bad Debt: The term bad debt refers as debt which is enable to collect from its debt holder. It is treated as a loss. If a business is having difficulties collecting money owed from one of its customers it may decide to cancel the debt. This is called a write-off and the accounts would need to be adjusted for this write-off.

Bad Debts Account: An account in the *nominal* ledger to record the value of un-recoverable debts from customers. Real bad debts are likely to happen can be deducted as expenses against tax liability.

Bad Debts Reserve Account: An account used to record an estimate of bad debts for the year usually as a percentage of sales. This cannot be deducted as an expense against tax liability.

Balance Brought Down: The difference between both sides of an account that is entered below the totals on the opposite side to the one on which the balance carried down was entered. Normally abbreviated to 'balance b/d'.

Balance Carried Down: The difference between both sides of an account that is entered above the totals and makes both sides equal to each other. Normally abbreviated to 'balance c/d'.

Balanced Scorecard: It is a technique that assesses performance across a balanced set of four perspectives – customers, internal processes, organizational learning and growth, and financial.

Balance of the Account: Balance of the account refers as insert the difference called a 'balance' between the two sides of an account, then total and rule of the account. Normally, done at the end of a period (usually a month, a quarter, or a year).

Balance Sheet: A report that details the various assets and liabilities of a business at a point in time, usually the end of an accounting period. It must balance, i.e., debits must always equal the credits. It is also called as a financial statement of the concern. In simple it is a statement which is prepared to know the financial position of the concern.

Bank Cash Book: A cash book that only contains entries relating to payments into and out of the bank.

Bank Loan: An amount of money advanced by a bank that has a fixed rate of interest is charged on the full amount, and is repayable by a specified future date.

Bank Payment: A transaction posted that reflects the payment for goods or a service where there has either been no invoice or the invoice is paid as soon as it is received thereby removing the need to post an invoice onto the purchase ledger.

Bank Receipt: A transaction posted that reflects the receipt of money for goods or a service where there has either been no invoice or the invoice is paid as soon as it is received thereby removing the need to post an invoice onto the sales ledger.

Bank Reconciliation: The process of matching and comparing figures from accounting records against those presented on a bank statement. The balance of the accounting ledger should reconcile/match to the balance of the bank statement.

Bank Reconciliation Statement: Bank reconciliation statement is a statement which comparing the Cash Book balance with the bank statement balance.

Bank Statement: A copy issued by a bank to a customer showing the customer's current account maintained at the bank.

Bankrupt: In simple, bankrupt means insolvent. A person, firm, or corporation that has been declared insolvent through a court proceeding and is relieved from the payment of all debts after the surrender of all assets to a court-appointed trustee.

Bankruptcy Order: When the court order making an individual bankrupt called as bankruptcy order.

Bill of Materials (BoM): A list of the other products (or components) that are needed to makeup a product. For example, a tool kit may have a bill of materials listing the following components — a tool box, a spanner set and a screwdriver.

Bid Price: A bid price is the highest price that a buyer (i.e., bidder) is willing to pay for a good. It is usually referred to simply as the "bid". In the context of stock exchange the bid price is the highest price a buyer of a stock is willing to pay for a share of that given stock. But on the other hand, the ask or offer price on the other hand is the lowest price a seller of a particular stock is willing to sell a share of that given stock.

Bidder: The person who has placed a bid in the book building process.

Bonus Shares: When the shares issued to existing shareholders free of charge called as bonus shares. It is also known as scrip issues. Bonus can be paid either in cash or in the form of *shares.* Cash bonus is paid by the company when it has large accumulated profits as well as cash to pay dividend. Many a time, a company is not in a position to pay bonus in cash in spite of sufficient profits because of unsatisfactory cash position or because of its adverse effects on the *working capital* of the company. In such a position, the company pays a bonus to its shareholders in the form of shares is known as a **bonus share.**

Bookkeeping: The process of keeping the records of data relating to accounting transactions in the accounting books, or software known as bookkeeping.

Books of Prime Entry: The books in which the details of the organization's transactions are initially recorded prior to entry into the main ledger.

Books of Original Entry: Books where the first entry recording a transaction is made. Sometimes, it also referred to as books of prime entry.

Break Even Point: The level of activity at which total revenues equal total costs called as break even point.

Budget: A forecast of expected income or expenditure over a specified period of time known as budget.

Business Entity Concept: Assumption that only transactions that affect the business and not the owner's private transactions will be recorded. For the accounting transaction business and owner are two separate hand.

Business-to-business (B2B): Businesses purchase from other businesses and/or sell their goods and services to other businesses.

Business-to-customer (B2C): Business-to-customer refers as businesses which sell to consumers.

Burn Rate: The rate at which a company spends its money. Example: if a company had cash reserves of $120m and it was currently spending $10m a month, you could say that the current 'burn rate' the company will run out of cash in one year.

By-product: By-product means products of minor sales value that result from the production of a main product.

B Share: B shares receive shares as a form of income, instead of dividends and are therefore attractive to investors who have to pay a high rate of income tax.

Bank Base Rate: The bank base rate is set by the Bank of England and determines the cost of borrowing money. This base rate is used by commercial banks as a reference point when setting their own base rates. An increase in the base rate will increase the rates for mortgages and loans. However, savers will receive higher interest rates on their savings.

Basis Point: The basis point refers as a hundredth of one per cent (0.01 per cent).

Bear Market: It arises when the security prices are a widespread decline and bears believe that share prices will fall. They sell securities which they do not at present own, in the hope that they can buy them at a lower price later once the price has fallen.

Beta: It is a tool to measure of systemic risk. It determines how volatile a share price is? The beta measures the distance between the high points and the low points, so the higher a share's beta, the more volatile it is.

Bid-offer Spread: It is also known as bid-ask or buy-sell spread. The bid-offer spread for securities such as *stock, futures contracts, options, or currency pairs* is the difference between the price quoted by a *market maker* for an immediate sale (bid) and an immediate purchase (ask). In simple, the offer price is what you pay if you want to buy an investment and the bid price is what you get when you want to sell. The difference between the offer price and the bid price is known as the spread.

Big Bang: The deregulation of the London Stock Market that took place in October 1986, when the London Stock Exchange went fully electronic.

Blue Chip: In general the term blue chip means large and creditworthy company in the market.

Bond: A bond is a long-term. debt. This a loan to a company or government in return for a fixed level of income (coupon) and a guaranteed return of the investment at the end of the bond's life (known as 'the maturity date').

Book Value: It is an accounting term and a company is determined the book value by adding up all of the company's assets and then deducting all of its debt and liabilities. The book value of a company's assets or securities may have little relationship to the market value of the company.

Bridging Loan: A short-term loan to provide temporary financing until more permanent financing is arranged. It is often used by purchasers of a property who need funds for a limited period of time.

Broker: A person who do the act of intermediary selling financial products.

Bull Market: It arises when the security prices is a widespread rise. A 'bull' investor believes that share prices will rise and they buy securities in the hope that they will be able to sell them at a profit later once the price has risen

Buyback: A company may buyback its own shares in order to reduce the overall number of shares available on the market. This will usually have the effect of increasing the share price.

Buyout: When a company's management team buys all the company's shares and takes complete control of the company called a Management Buy-out (MBO).There are several variants of any MBO.

- **Leverage buyout** — These occur where the purchase price is beyond the financial resources of the managers and the bulk of the acquisition is financed by loan capital provided by other investors.

- **Employee buyout** — When all employees are offered a stake in the new business is called employee buyout.

C

Call: When shares are issued only part of their cost is usually paid at the time of application and allotment. A "call" is a demand by the company for part or all of the outstanding sums to be paid.

Called Up Share Capital: The face value of shares for which payment has been requested to the shareholder.

Capital: In general, capital is the money invested in the business. Shareholder's capital employed refers to share capital and reserves only.

Capital Employed: Capital employed is usually represented as *fixed assets plus current assets* minus *current liabilities* or *non-current assets* plus *working capital.*

Capital Employed = Total Assets "Current Liabilities"

Capital Expenditure: Capital expenditure is the expenditure which is generally incurred for long period. Expenditure incurred on the acquisition of an asset, such as premises, motor vehicles, plant or machinery that will be used within the business over a period of years.

Capital Gain: Profit made on selling an asset for more than its original purchase price.

Capital Gains Tax: Tax paid on the profit made on selling an asset for more than its original purchase price, i.e., the capital gain.

Capitalization: Capitalization/market capitalization/market cap is a measurement of size of a business enterprise or corporation equal to the *share price* times the number of *shares outstanding* of a *public company.* Capitalization could represent the public opinion of a company's *networth* and is a determining factor in *stock valuation.* It also the sum of a *corporation's long-term debt, stock* and *retained earnings* also called ***invested capital.*** The *market price* of an entire *company,* calculated by multiplying the number of *shares outstanding* by the *price per share.*

Capital Redemption Reserve: A 'non-distributable' reserve created when shares are redeemed or purchased other than from the proceeds of a fresh issue of shares called as capital redemption reserve.

Capital Reserve: It is that part of shareholders' funds that comes from accumulated capital surpluses. For example, an upward revaluation of capital assets. The term is also used in everyday sense to refer to accumulated surplus profits.

Carriage Inwards: Carriage inwards means the cost of transport of goods into a business.

Carriage Outwards: Carriage outwards means the cost of transport of goods out to the customers of a business.

Cash Book: It is a book used to record details of cash moving in and out of the bank current account.

Cash Flow: Cash flow refers to the movement of cash into or out of a business, a project, or a financial product. It is usually measured during a specified period of time.

Cash Flow Statement: In financial accounting, a cash flow statement also known as ***statement of cash flows*** or ***funds flow statement.*** The cash flow statement is concerned with the flow of cash in and cash out of the business. As an analytical tool, the statement of cash flows is useful in determining the short-term viability of a company.

Cash Payment: A transaction posted that reflects the payment for goods or a service where there has either been no invoice or the invoice is paid as soon as it is received thereby removing the need to post an invoice onto the purchase ledger.

Cash Receipt: A transaction posted that reflects the receipt of money for goods or a service where there has either been no invoice or the invoice is paid as soon as it is received thereby removing the need to post an invoice onto the sales ledger.

Charge Card: It is one type of payment card that requires the cardholder to settle the account in full at the end of the specified period; e.g., American Express and Diners Cards. Holders have to pay an annual fee for the card.

Chart of Accounts: A list of all the nominal accounts used by a business and used to analyze income, expenditure, assets, liabilities and capital; together with the way such categories are assigned to the Balance Sheet or Profit and Loss report.

Clearing: The process by which amounts paid by cheque from an account in one bank are transferred to the bank account of the payee.

Close of Account: Close of account means totalling and ruling of an account on which there is no outstanding balance.

Closing Balance: The balance of an account at the end of an accounting period and the balancing figure is then carried forward to the next accounting period.

Columnar Purchase Day Book: A purchase day book used to record all items obtained on credit and it has analysis columns so that various types of expenditure can be grouped together in a column. It also called a purchases analysis book.

Columnar Sales Day Book: A sales day book used to show the all credit sales for a period and organized in analysis columns according to how the information recorded is to be analyzed. It also called a sales analysis book.

Compensating Error: Error in computation or in recording of *accounting data* that is neutralized (counter balanced) by an equal and opposite error. Since compensating *errors* do not show up in the total, they are difficult to locate through *statistical methods.*

Compound Interest: Compound interest is the interest earned during a period calculated on the basis of the original sum together with interest earned from previous periods. If the compound interest is C%, and the original investment is ₹ P, then the value of the investment after n years is:

₹P × ((100 + c)/100)n

Consistency: Keeping to the same method or recording and processing business transactions known as consistency.

Consolidation Accounting: This term means bringing together into a single balance sheet and profit and loss accounts the separate financial statements of a group of companies. It also known as group financial statements.

Contra Entry: The adjustment made to balance transactions in one ledger with another. The most common type of contra entry is balancing outstanding purchase ledger transactions against outstanding sales ledger transactions where both sell to and buy from the same company.

Contribution: Contribution means the difference between sales income and marginal cost/variable cost. C= Sales – Variable cost

Corporation Tax: A form of direct taxation levied on the profits of companies. The rate is determined each year in the Finance Act.

Cost Centre: A production or service location, function, activity, or item of equipment whose costs may be attributed to cost units.

Cost of Sales/Cost of Goods Sold: In general term Cost of Goods Sold refers as the direct costs attributable to the production of goods sold by a company. This includes material cost and direct labour cost and excludes indirect cost like advertising or R&D. COGS appear on the income statement. Method of calculating cost of goods sold is: **Opening stock + Purchase of goods – Closing stock.**

Cost Unit: A unit of product or service in relation to which costs are ascertained.

Credit: One side of the double-entry bookkeeping process, representing negative figures on the balance sheet reductions in assets; increases in liabilities and capital, and income on the profit and loss report.

Credit Card: A credit card is a small plastic card issued to users of a system of payment. It allows its holder to buy goods and services up to a pre-arranged limit based on the holder's promise to pay for these goods and services.

Credit Note: In simple credit note means, sent from the seller to the customer when goods are returned, in order to cancel or reverse all or part of an invoice. It also named as **credit memorandum or credit memo** issued by a seller to a buyer.

Creditors: Third parties to whom money is owed by the business.

Current Account: A bank account used for regular payments in and out of the bank.

Current Asset: A current asset is an asset that's worth can be easily realized. For example, money in the bank or in petty cash, debtors, prepayments, or stock.

Current Liability: A current liability is a debt owed by the company with the short period of time. For example, creditors, accruals or an overdraft that will be cleared in the short-term.

Current Ratio: The current ratio is a financial ratio that measures whether or not a firm has enough resources to meet *short-term debt obligations.* The higher the *ratio,* the more *liquid* the *company* is. If the current *assets* of a company are more than twice the current *liabilities,* then that company is generally considered to have good *short-term financial strength.*

Current Ratio = Current Assets ÷ Current Liabilities

C Shares: A class of share issued by the investment trusts that carries an ongoing fee.

Call Option: An option that gives the holder the right to buy shares at a specified price on a specified date in the future.

Capital Growth: The term capital growth means the increase in value of assets and investments.

Charting: Chartists believe that investment opportunities can be spotted by analyzing changes in share price trends.

Churning: The term used to describe the excessive trading of a client's account by a broker in order to increase their commissions.

Commission: The charge made by a stockbroker or the fee a financial adviser makes from a company whose products have been sold, generally based on the value of the sale.

Commodities: Commodity markets are markets where raw or primary products are exchanged. These raw commodities are traded on regulated commodities exchanges, in which they are bought and sold in standardized contracts.

Company Share Option Scheme: A scheme offered by companies to employees to encourage better performance. Participants are given the right to buy shares in the company in the future, usually at a discount.

Contract Note: Contract note is a statement to know the confirmation of share purchase transaction.

Convertible Bonds or Loan Stock: Bonds/loan stock that gives the holder the right to convert to shares at a future date. The aim is to give investors a regular income whilst also giving them the chance to share in the capital growth of the company at a later date. It is a hybrid security with debt- and equity-like features.

Corporate Bond: The bonds issued by a public company to the general public is called a corporate bond.

Coupon: The interest rate on a fixed-interest security.

Crest: The electronic system for settling share transactions, introduced in July 1997 by the London Stock Exchange, under which paper share certificates are no longer needed.

Cum Dividend: If a dividend is just about to be paid on a share then an investor buying a cum dividend share will be entitled to receive the dividend. If the share is ex-dividend, it means the dividend has already been paid out.

D

Day Book: A day book is a book that lists all transactions in the order that they arise. A day book for different types of transaction, e.g., a sales day book, a purchase day book, etc.

Debenture: The term debenture is used when a limited company receives money on loan, and certificates called debenture certificates are issued to the lender. Interest will be paid to the holder, the rate of interest being shown on the certificate. In simple, it is a acknowledgement of debt.

Debit: The left hand side of the double entry process, representing positive figures on the balance sheet (increases in assets; reductions in liabilities and capital), and expenditures on the profit and loss report.

Debit Card: A card linked to a bank account and used to pay for goods and services by debiting the holders account. It usually combined with other facilities such as ATM and cheque guarantee card functions.

Debit Note: Debit note is a *letter* issued by a *seller* to the customer the *amount* owed by them. An invoice is a type of debit note. It is also called debit memo.

Debtors: A debtor is an entity that owes a debt to someone else and it may be an individual, a firm, a government, a company or other legal person. The debtor is more often referred to as a borrower.

Debtors' Prison: A debtor's prison is a prison for those who are unable to pay a debt.

Depletion: An accounting term describing the amortization of assets that can be physically reduced. For example, coal mines, oil fields and other natural resources are depleted on company accounting statements.

Deposit Account: A bank account for money to be kept in for a long time. Normally, pay a higher rate of interest as compared to a current account.

Depreciation: In simple depreciation means decreasing the value of a fixed asset, due to use, obsolescence, etc., in the calculation of net profit.

Direct Costs: Director costs are those costs that can be traced to the item being manufactured directly.

Direct Expenses: Direct expenses are those expenses that are incurred in the actual manufacture and sale of the product or the sale and provision of the service, i.e., the expenses incurred by the business actually trading. For example, the wages of the machine operators, the power to run the machines, the wages and commission of the sales staff, the cost of advertising and any sales promotions.

Directors: Director is a person who officials appointed by shareholders to manage the company for them.

Discount: The amount by which a bill is reduced and can be given for a variety of reasons, e.g., buying in bulk, spending large amounts, being a preferred customer (trade discounts) or settlement discount.

Discount Allowed: A deduction from the amount due, given to the customers, who pay their accounts within the time allowed. It appears as an expense in the profit and loss account.

Discount Received: A deduction from the amount due, given to a business, by a supplier, when their account is paid before the time allowed has elapsed. It appears as income in the profit and loss part of the trading and the profit and loss account.

Dishonoured Cheque: A cheque which the drawer's bank has refused to make payment upon.

Dissolution: When the relation between all the partners of the firm comes to an end, this is called dissolution of the firm.

Dividend: It is one type of cash reward to the shareholder upon their investment in form of share given by the company out of profits.

Double Entry: A system of bookkeeping in which every transaction of a business is entered as a debit in one account and as a credit in another. Every transaction must have an equal or zero effect on both sides of the accounting equation.

Drawee: The *party* directed to *pay* the *amount* of a *draft* or cheque. In simple, who will have to pay the funds to the payee.

Drawer: Drawer is the person who is writing and signing a cheque

Drawings: Cash or goods taken from the business for the owner's personal use. It applies only to sole traders and partnerships. It does not count as an expense in the profit and loss account and must be included in the financial section of the balance sheet.

Dual Aspect Concept: This state that there are two aspects of accounting, one represented by the assets of the business and the other by the claims against them. The concept states that these two aspects are always equal to each other. In other words, this is the alternate form of the accounting equation:

Assets = Liabilities + Capital

Dual aspect concept is known as "Double Entry Bookkeeping System".

Day Trading: The trade of buying and selling stocks by individuals known as day traders during a trading day. The aim is to make a profit on the day and not hold stocks at the close of the trading session.

Deflation: The rate at which the general level of prices for goods and services is decreasing. It is opposite of the inflation.

Dematerialization: The increase in electronic technology and the introduction of systems, such as, crest in the stock exchange has meant that paper share certificates are no longer needed. Instead ownership of shares can be logged electronically in a crest account and contract notes, confirmation of share transactions, can be sent electronically.

Demutualization: The process of changing the legal structure of a company from a mutual form of ownership to a stock form of ownership.

Depositary Receipt: A certificate which gives the holder, ownership of a specified number of shares in a company that have been deposited with a financial institution.

Derivatives: An agreement between two parties — that has a value determined by the price of something, i.e., called the underlying which involves the right to buy or sell the underlying instrument at an agreed price. The value of a derivative instrument depends on the value of another asset.

Discount Rate: Discount rate is the rate used to calculate the present value of future cash flows.

Discounted Rate Mortgage: A mortgage which guarantees that the interest rate charged will be lower than the lender's standard variable rate. The lower rate offered is usually set for a specified period of time and reverts to the standard rate after that period.

Discretionary Management: A broker who has authority to execute all decisions regarding stocks and shares on behalf of his client without getting prior approval.

Distribution: The term distribution generally refers as the payment of dividends to shareholders from the company's profits.

Dividend Yield: The dividend yield is the return getting for investing in a company and it is calculated by dividing the dividend by the current share price, expressed as a percentage. The gross dividend yield is used in preference to the net dividend yield, so that investors can make a direct comparison with gross interest yields from loan stocks and gilts.

Dow Jones Industrial Average: 'The Dow' is one of the main USA share indices which monitors the performance of 30 industrial companies traded on the New York Stock Exchange.

E

Economic Order Quantity (EOQ): A mathematical method of calculating the amount of stock that should be ordered at a time and how frequently to order it, so that the overall total of the costs of holding the stock and the costs of ordering the stock can be minimized.

Endorsement: A means by which someone may pass the right to collect money on a cheque.

Enterprise Resource Planning (ERP) System: A suite of software modules, each of which relates to a function of the organization, such as order processing, production, creditor control, debtor control, payroll, marketing, and human resources.

Equity: In simple the equity refers as the net assets or worth of a company after all creditors have been paid-off.

Equity Accounting: A method of accounting whereby a corporation will document a portion of the undistributed profits for an affiliated company in which they own a position. In simple it is a process of accounting for associated undertakings that brings into the consolidated profit and loss account the investor's share of the associated undertaking's results and that records the investment in the consolidated balance sheet as the investor's share of the associated undertaking's net assets.

Error of Commission: Where a correct amount is entered, but in the wrong persons account.

Error of Omission: Where a transaction is completely omitted from the books of accounts.

Error of Original Entry: Where an item is entered, but both the debit and credit entries are of the same incorrect amount.

Error of Principle: Where an item is entered in the wrong type of account, e.g., a fixed asset in an expense account.

Exception Reporting: A process of issuing a warning message to decision-makers when something unexpected is happening: for example, when expenditure against a budget is higher than it should be.

Expenses: An **expense** or **expenditure** is an outflow of money to another person or group to pay for an item or service, or for a category of costs. For a tenant, rent is an expense. But in simple language any *cost* of doing *business* resulting from revenue-generating activities.

Early-redemption Penalty: A financial penalty that is levied by mortgage lenders for switching to another lender and payable on certain types of loans, such as, discount and fixed-interest rate loans upon early redemption or part redemption during the specified early redemption period.

Earnings Per Share (EPS)

The EPS is calculated by dividing the earnings (pre-tax profits) by the number of shares in issue. It is one of the key ratios is used in the valuation of shares as it expresses the amount of profit a company manages to make per share.

Emerging Markets: The term emerging markets means growing market. The stock markets based in developing countries that have a low income per head compared with the developed world. These are attractive markets for speculative investors in the Western countries because there is potential for rapid economic growth but at a higher economic and political risk.

Endowment Policy: A policy which combines investment with insurance and runs for a specific period. It builds up a cash value, generally on either a with profit or with unit-linked basis and is paid out at the end of the policy term or when you die (whichever is the earliest).

Enhanced Scrip Dividend: A dividend that is in the form of shares rather than cash and to encourage shareholders to take the scrip dividend the value of the shares is usually greater than the cash dividend.

Equity Capital: In simple it is called as owner's capital. The owners of the equity capital are collectively the owners of the company and they are the risk bearing shareholders as they benefit from capital growth if the share price rises but bear the highest risk if the company is wound up.

Ethical Investments: Investments that are made in companies that make a positive contribution to the world and are kind to the environment. Most ethical investments are made through a managed investment fund such as a unit trust or pension fund, as it is difficult for an individual investor to judge whether a particular company is ethical or not.

Euro: The Euro is Europe's new unit of currency that was officially launched in January 1999 in eleven countries in the European Union. All of the national notes and coins in the relevant countries will ceased to be legal tender by the end of February 2002; however, banks will continue to accept them until 2004.

Euro Sterling Bond: Euro sterling bond is a corporate bond issued by a UK company that wants to raise money in the international markets instead of its home market.

Ex-dividend: A share sold without the right to the next declared dividend payment.

Execution Only: A type of share dealing service where the customer makes his or her own investment decision and the stock broker just carries out the transaction.

Exercise Price: The price at which the underlying security can be purchased (call option) or sold (put option). The exercise price is determined at the time the option contract is formed.

Exit Charge: Exit charge is one type of payment that has to be made by an investor selling an investment.

Extraordinary General Meeting (EGM): A meeting called either by the Board of Directors or shareholders of a company to discuss special business and it include matters, such as, a proposed takeover or merger, or a substantial change in the way the business is to be run.

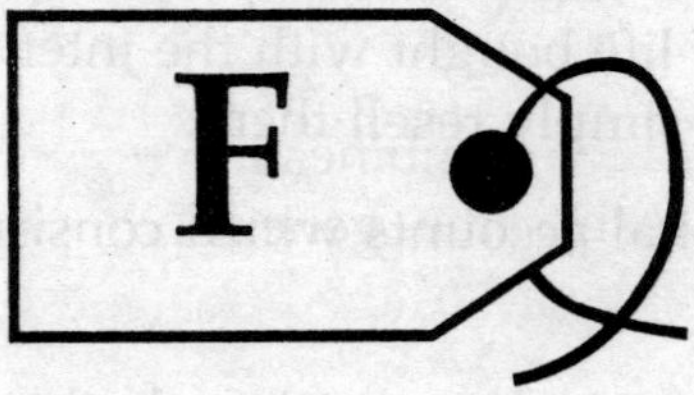

Factoring: Factoring is a financial transaction whereby a business sells its accounts receivable, i.e., invoices to a third party called a factor at a discount in exchange for immediate money with which to finance continued business.

Fallacy of Omission: Leaving out information that is relevant but that could weaken your position.

Favourable Variance: A difference arising that is apparently 'good' from the perspective of the organization. For example, when the total actual labour cost is less than the total standard cost.

FIFO: FIFO stands for first-in-first-out, meaning that the oldest inventory items are recorded as sold first. It is an accounting methods for managing inventory and financial matters involving the money a company tied up within inventory of produced goods, raw materials, parts, components, or feed stocks. So, the costs of items in stock always reflect the most recent purchases.

Floor Price: The term floor price means the minimum offer price below which bids cannot be entered. The issuer company in consultation with the book running lead managers fixes the floor price.

Final Accounts: It refers to statements produced at the end of accounting periods, such as the trading and profit and loss account and the balance sheet. Nowadays, the term 'financial statements' is more commonly used.

Finance Lease: An agreement whereby the lessee enjoys substantially all the risks and rewards associated with ownership of an asset other than legal title.

Financial Accounting: Financial accounting is concerned with recording financial transactions which already happened and with providing information from the accounting records, for example in order to prepare VAT returns, and trial balance (the starting point for the preparation of the profit and loss statement and balance sheet).

Financial Modelling: Financial modelling is the process of manipulating accounting data to generate forecasts and perform sensitivity analysis.

Fixed Assets: Assets which the business intends to retain for the coming year rather than convert into cash. Typical fixed assets include property, office equipment, motor vehicle, etc. Assets which have a long life bought with the intention to use them in the business and not with the intention to simply resell them.

Fixed Capital Accounts: Capital accounts which consist only of the amounts of capital actually paid into the firm.

Fixed Costs: Expenses which remain constant whether activity rises or falls, within a given range of activity.

Flexible Budget: A flexible budget is a budget which is changeable in by the nature. A budget which, by recognizing the difference in behaviour between fixed and variable costs in relation to fluctuations in output, turnover or other factors, is designed to change appropriately with such fluctuations.

Fluctuating Capital Accounts: Capital accounts whose balances change from one period to the next is called as fluctuating capital accounts.

Folio Columns: Columns used for entering reference numbers.

Forecasting: Taking present data and expected future trends, such as growth of a market and anticipated changes in price levels and demand, in order to arrive at a view of what the likely economic position of a business will be at some future date.

Face Value: The term used to describe value of a bond when it matures, also known as the 'nominal' or 'par' value.

Fee-based Adviser: An independent financial adviser who earns a living by charging a fee for advice rather than earning commission from financial companies for selling their products.

Final Dividend: The final dividend is paid after the annual accounts for the year have been published and after the proposed dividend has been agreed by the shareholders at the annual general meeting.

Financial Services Act, 1986: The Financial Services Act, 1986 has established regulations for firms in the investment service industry, including buying and selling of stocks. It has now been overtaken by the Financial Services and Markets Act, 2000 has centralized regulatory power in the hands of the Financial Services Authority.

Financial Services Authority (FSA): The single statutory financial regulator in UK. In order to do business in UK most financial service firms must get permission from the FSA. The FSA regulates banks, building societies, credit unions, insurance and investment firms and independent financial advisers.

Financial Times Stock Exchange 100 Index (FTSE 100): The FTSE 100 index is a share price index for 100 different shares quoted on the London stock exchange. The shares are intended to be of a sufficiently broad cross section, so that movements in the index of share prices would be typical of movements in the value of the portfolio of shares of an average investor.

Fixed Interest Security: A fixed interest security is an investment which has a return consisting of income in the form of interest payments and either a redemption value of the security when it eventually matures or the market value of the security if the investor sells it before maturity.

Fixed-rate Mortgage: A mortgage where the rate of interest is fixed for a set period of time. The advantage of this type of mortgage is that the investor can budget accurately.

Flexible Mortgage: A new type of mortgage that is becoming more popular, especially among the self-employed and other people who may experience uneven cash flow. It allows you to vary your monthly payments without any penalty and can also borrow, or 'draw down', from the loan when you need to and the ability to over pay can save you a lot of interest over the term of the loan.

Flotation or Floatation: Flotation is the process of making a company's shares available to the general public by obtaining a quotation on the stock exchange and also referred to as "going public" or "obtaining a stock exchange listing".

Front-end Loading: The initial sales charges that have to pay when invest in a mutual fund, such as, a unit trust. This charge is mainly for the cost of the adviser.

Future: A form of forward contract to buy or sell a set quantity of shares or commodities in the future at a preagreed price.

G

Garner V. Murrary Rule: This rule says that when a partnership firm is dissolved at that time, first of all, all partners shall bring the realization loss in cash in their profit sharing ratio. If any partner is found insolvent then the solvent partners who have credit balance in their capital Accounts shall bear the loss of the insolvent partner in their profit sharing ratio.

General Ledger: The general ledger, sometimes known as the nominal ledger. It is the main accounting record of a business which uses double entry bookkeeping and usually include accounts for such items as current assets, fixed assets, liabilities, revenue and expense items, gains and losses.

Going Concern Concept: The assumption that a business is to continue for the foreseeable future.

Goodwill: An intangible asset of a business reflecting its commercial reputation, customer connections, etc.

Gross Equity Accounting: A form of equity accounting applicable to joint ventures under which the investor's share of the aggregate gross assets and liabilities of the joint venture is shown on the face of the balance sheet and the investor's share of the joint venture's turnover is noted in the profit and loss account.

Gross Loss: When the cost of goods sold exceeds the sales revenue generally called as gross loss.

Gross Margin: A measure of the profitability of a business by which the gross profit is divided by the sales. It is usually expressed as a percentage.

Gross Profit: The difference between total revenue from sales and the total cost of purchases or materials, with an adjustment for stock.

Gearing: Gearing is the ratio of a company's debt to its assets and measures the financial risk of a company's capital structure. Due to the financial risk associated with gearing, higher gearing will increase the rate of return required by investors. Gearing is called leverage in US.

Gilt: Secure bonds issued by UK government also known as 'gilt edged securities' or 'fixed interest securities'. Gilts are bought at their par value or at face value. Most gilts are 'dated' which means that at a fixed date in the future, the par value will be repaid to the investor.

Gross: The gross amount is the amount before the deduction of tax.

Gross Redemption Yield: The return on a fixed interest security expressed as an annual percentage. The redemption yield consists of the capital and income return on the investment.

Gross Yield: The gross yield on an investment is the annual gross dividend or income received expressed as a percentage. The gross yield is used in preference to the net yield, because investors can make a direct comparison with (gross) interest yields from other loan stocks and gilts.

Guaranteed Income Bond: A single premium insurance bond which pays out a fixed amount of annual income and returns the original sum invested at maturity.

H

Hire Purchase Agreements: In simple it is called as instalment buying. It is the legal term for a contract, in these persons usually agrees to pay for goods in parts or a percentage at a time. It was developed in the United Kingdom and can now found in China, Japan, Malaysia, India, Australia, and New Zealand. It is also called closed-end leasing. In general it is a legal agreement by which an organization can obtain the use of an asset in exchange for payment by instalment.

Historical Cost Concept: Historical cost concept means the assets are normally shown at cost price.

Holding Company: A holding company is a company or firm that hold maximum voting power of other companies. It usually refers to a company which does not produce goods or services itself; rather its only purpose is owning shares of other companies.

Honorarium: A voluntary fee paid for a service which is usually free.

Hedging: A hedging is a position established in one market in an attempt to offset exposure to price fluctuations in some opposite position in another market with the goal of minimizing one's exposure to unwanted risk. There are many specific financial vehicles to accomplish this, including insurance policies, forward contracts, options, etc., perfect hedge produces a riskless portfolio.

I

Ideal Standard: A standard that is based upon the premise that everything operates at the maximum level of efficiency. It takes no account of normal losses, or of normal levels of downtime and waste.

Impersonal Accounts: All accounts other than the personal accounts called as impersonal account. Impersonal account generally categorieses as real and nominal accounts.

Imprest System: The imprest system is a form of financial accounting system and the most common imprest system is the petty cash system. The base characteristic of an imprest system is that a fixed amount is reserved, which will be replenished at the end of a period or when the circumstances request it. This replenishment is not credited on the imprest account, but from another source.

Income and Expenditure Account: An account for a non-profit-oriented organization to find the surplus or deficit made during a period.

Indirect Manufacturing Costs: Costs relating to manufacture that cannot be economically traced to the item being manufactured. It also known as 'indirect costs' and sometimes, as 'factory overhead expenses'.

Input Tax: When a company registered for value added tax (VAT) buys goods or services from another supplier, VAT is charged. This is known as input tax.

Inputs: In simple inputs means the purchases of goods and services.

Intangible Assets: Intangible assets are those assets which is invisible by the nature. It include copyrights, patents, goodwill, etc., they are salable but do not contain any intrinsic productive value.

Interest: It is one type of charge made on a loan or money received on a capital investment.

Interest on Capital: An amount at an agreed rate of interest which is credited to a partner based on the amount of capital contributed by him/her.

Interest on Drawings: An amount at an agreed rate of interest, based on the drawings taken out, which is debited to the partners.

Invoice: An invoice or bill is a commercial document issued by a seller to the buyer, indicating the products, quantities, and agreed prices for products or services the seller has provided the buyer. It indicates the buyer must pay the seller, according to the payment terms. The buyer has a maximum amount of days to pay these goods and are sometimes offered a discount if paid before.

Irrelevant Costs: It is a managerial accounting term that represents a cost, either positive or negative, that does not relate to a situation requiring management's decision.

Income Share: Class of share within a split capital investment trust that receives a high dividend yield.

Indemnity Insurance: An insurance which is designed to protect a mortgage lender against the risk of you defaulting or not being able to repay the mortgage. The policy is usually imposed upon by the lender at the start of the loan and the premium payable is determined by the level of perceived risk to the home lender of you defaulting on the loan.

Index-linked Investment: An investment that increases in value each year by the rate of inflation or by a fixed percentage above inflation. Index-linking is mostly associated with income-producing investments, such as, government issued gilts.

Inflation: The general increase in prices overtime and effect of reducing the buying power of money. The most common measure of inflation is the Retail Prices Index (RPI).

Initial Public Offering (IPO): An initial public offering (IPO) referred to simply as an "offering" or "flotation," is when a company issues common stock or shares to the public for the first time. In simple when a new share issue by a company coming to the stock market for the first time.

Insider Dealing or Insider Trading: It refers to the illegal use of privileged information which, if made public, would significantly affect the share price. For example, if someone knows that a company is about to make an announcement which will affect the price of its shares; it would be an insider dealing if he/she uses that information to buys or sells shares in advance of the announcement to make a profit.

Interest Cover: The number of times the interest payments on debt can be covered by the company's profits.

Investment Trust: Investment trusts are companies whose business is to investment in the securities of a wide range of other companies. Like unit trusts, they pool together the money of many investors in order to invest it in a portfolio of companies which will be more varied than what small investors could achieve on their own.

J

Job Costing: A costing system that is applied when goods or services are produced in discrete jobs, either one item at a time, or in batches.

Job Product: Two or more products, each of which has significant sales value, created in the same production process.

Joint Ventures: When two businesses join together for a set of activities and agree to share the profits.

Journal Entries: In accounting, a journal entry is a logging of transactions into accounting journal items. It can consist of several items, each of which is either a debit or a credit. Sometimes referred to as a 'Journal'.

Joint Life Annuity: An annuity that continues after the death of the first partner and ends after the death of the second partner.

Junk Bond: A junk bond is a high-risk, non-investment-grade *bond* with a *low* credit rating, it is the opposite of *investment-grade bond.*

L

Ledgers: A ledger is the principal book for recording of business transactions. The details of customers and their transactions are recorded in the sales ledger; suppliers and their transactions are recorded in the purchase ledger. All ledgers are amalgamated in the nominal ledger by the posting of balances from the individual ledgers.

Liabilities: Amounts owed by a business to third parties including suppliers, banks, tax authorities and employees.

LIBID: The London Interbank Bid Rate (LIBID) is a bid rate; the rate bid by banks on Eurocurrency deposits (i.e., the rate at which a bank is willing to borrow from other banks).

LIBOR: London Interbank Offered Rate (LIBOR, pronounced LIE-bore) is a daily reference rate based on the interest rates at which banks offer to lend unsecured funds to other banks in the London wholesale money market. LIBOR will be slightly higher than the London Interbank Bid Rate (LIBID), the rate at which banks are prepared to accept deposits.

LIFO: LIFO stands for last-in-first-out, meaning that the most recently purchased items are recorded as sold first.

Limited Company: A limited company is a company with shareholders whose liability is limited by shares, which is the most common form of privately held company. Most large businesses will be formed as limited companies. A limited company may be "private" or "public".

Limited Liability: A limited liability means the liability of the members are limited up to the value of their share. If the business of a sole trader or a partnership is declared bankrupt then the owner or owners are personally liable for any outstanding debts of the business. However, the shareholders of a company have limited liability. They will lose is the amount they paid for their shares.

Limited Partner: A partner whose liability is limited to the capital he or she has put into the firm.

Liquidity: A measure of the ability of a debtor to pay their debts as and when they fall due and usually expressed as a ratio or a percentage of current liabilities.

Liquidity Ratios: Those ratios that relate to the cash position in an organization and hence its ability to pay liabilities when due.

Loan: A loan is a type of debt. It is an arrangement in which a lender loans money or property known as the principal or principle amount to a borrower and the borrower agrees to return the property or repay the money, usually along with interest, at some future point in time.

Lodgement: A lodgement is an enclave taken by and defended by *force of arms* against determined opposition made by increasing the size of a bridgehead into a substantial defended area, the rear parts of which — at the least — are out of direct line of fire. In simple it refer as an accumulation or a deposit.

Long-term Liabilities: Liabilities that do not have to be paid within twelve months of the balance sheet date.

Leverage: Leverage also known as gearing or levering refers to the use of debt capital to supplement equity capital. A firm with significantly more debt than equity is considered to be highly leveraged.

Leveraged Buyout: Purchase of a company by an institution using a high proportion of debt. A type of Management Buyout (MBO).

Limit Order An order of instructions that an investor gives to his broker, which sets out the limits that he/she is prepared to pay for investments.

Limited-life Trust: A trust which has been set up for a limited period, after which it will be wound up.

Liquidation: The process of ending the existence of a company. A company will go into liquidation if it is unable to pay its debts. In this situation the company's assets will be sold in order to pay-off its debts.

Listed Company: A listed company is one whose shares are included in the official list of securities and are dealt with by members of the stock exchange.

Loan Stock: Long-term debt issued by a company in order to raise capital for which interest is paid.

London International Financial Futures and Options Exchange (LIFFOE): LIFFOE allows investors and business enterprises to use financial futures to speculate or to hedge against risks of movements in gilt prices, interest rates, foreign currency exchange rates, shares prices and bond prices.

Low-start Mortgage: A mortgage that offers a low interest rate initially which then rises to the lender's standard variable rate after a set date agreed at the start of the mortgage.

Loan to Value (LTV): The ratio between the size of the loan you are seeking and the mortgage lenders valuation of the property.

London Stock Exchange (LSE): The London stock exchange is a primary capital market in which companies and other institutions can raise funds by issuing shares or loan stock. However, it is more important as a secondary market for buying and selling existing securities.

M

Main Ledger: Main ledger is the ledger where the double-entry takes place of all transactions of the business.

Management Accounting: Management accounting or managerial accounting is concerned with the provisions and use of accounting information to managers within organizations, to provide them with the basis to make informed business decisions that will allow them to be better equipped in their management and control functions.

Manufacturing Account: A financial statement which shows production costs only and it will include direct materials and labour costs and the production overhead. In simple it refers an account in which production cost is calculated.

Margin: The purchase and sale of a good may be shown as Cost Price + Profit = Selling Price. The profit when expressed as a fraction, or percentage, of the selling price is known as the margin.

Margin of Safety: The gap between the level of activity at the break even point and the actual level of activity.

Marginal Costing: Marginal costing is also known as variable costing. Change in the total cost arises when the quantity produced changes by one unit, i.e., cost of producing one more unit of a good. It includes only variable costs i.e. direct materials, direct labour and variable overhead.

Mark-up: The purchase and sale of a good may be shown as Cost Price + Profit = Selling Price. The percentage added to the cost price to provide a profit is known as the mark-up.

Master Budget: In simple master budget is a summary of all individual budget.

Materiality Concept: The materiality concept is the principle that trivial matters are to be disregarded in accounting, and all important matters are to be disclosed. The materiality concept is an established, recognized accounting convention.

Memorandum Joint Venture Account: A memorandum account outside the double entry system where the information contained in all the joint venture accounts held by the parties to the joint ventures are collated, the joint venture profit is calculated and the share of profit of each party is recorded in order to close-off the account.

Merchant Banker: An entity registered under the Securities and Exchange Board of India (Merchant Bankers) Regulations, 1999.

Minority Interests: Minority interest in business is an accounting concept that refers to the portion of a subsidiary corporation's stock that is not owned by the parent corporation. The magnitude of the minority interest in the subsidiary company is always less than 50% of outstanding shares. Minority interest is an integral part of the enterprise value of a company.

Money Measurement Concept: The concept that accounting is concerned only with facts measurable in monetary terms, and for which purpose measurements can be used that obtain general agreement as to their suitability.

Market Capitalization: The market value of a company which is calculated by multiplying the number of shares in issue by the current price of the shares.

Market Maker: Dealers on the stock market who buy and sell stocks and shares on their own behalf to make a profit.

Maturity: Term used to describe the period when an investment comes to end, and, in the case of bonds, loan stock, or debentures, when the nominal capital is repaid to the holder and it also known as redemption.

Mortgage Indemnity Guarantee (MIG): An insurance which is designed to protect a mortgage lender against the risk of defaulting or not being able to repay the mortgage. The policy is usually imposed upon by the lender at the start of the loan and the premium payable is determined by the level of perceived risk defaulting on the loan.

Mortgage Protection Policy: A life insurance policy that pays off your mortgage if you were to die during the mortgage term.

Mutual Funds: A mutual fund is a professionally managed type of collective investment scheme that pools money from many investors and invests typically in investment securities (stocks, bonds, short-term money market instruments, or commodities). Unlike investment trusts mutual funds are open-end funds where the investor may redeem his/her shares at anytime at the prevailing market price.

N

Narrative: A description and explanation of the transaction recorded in the journal called as narrative or sometime it also called as narration.

Negative Contribution: The excess of direct costs allocated to a section of a business over the revenue from that section.

Negative Goodwill: The name given to the amount by which the total purchase price for a business of a limited company has taken over is less than the valuation of the assets. The amount is entered at the top of the fixed assets in the balance sheet as a negative amount.

Negotiation: In simplest terms, negotiation is a discussion between two or more disputants who are trying to workout a solution to their problem. Negotiations typically take place because the parties wish to resolve a problem or a dispute between them.

Net: The term net means the amount that remains after all deductions have been made.

Net Book Value (NBV): The net value of an asset. Equal to its original cost (its book value) minus depreciation and amortization. Also called net book value and depreciated cost.

Net Current Assets: Net Current Assets = Current Assets — Current Liabilities. Same as called working capital.

Net Loss: Where the cost of goods sold plus expenses is greater than the revenue.

Net Present Value (NPV): The sum of the present values of a series of cash flows.

Net Profit: The amount earned by a company after expenses. It calculated as;

Net Profit = Gross Profit – Expenses

Net Realizable Value (NRV): The amount that would be received for the immediate sale of stock, after accounting for any costs associated directly with the sale.

Net Worth: The value of a business as represented by subtracting its liabilities from its assets;

Assets – Liabilities = Net Worth

Nominal Account: Accounts which is not touchable and visible only to feel. It refers as all types of expenses, revenue and capital.

Nominal Ledger: A nominal ledger also known as a general ledger, or as speed codes or cost centers, allows to keep track of which areas of business generate what proportion of income and expenditure. Even in a small business, this can be useful for enabling management to decide which areas to concentrate on promoting, and where costs need to be better controlled.

Normal Losses: Losses arising in the production process that could not be avoided.

National Association of Securities Dealers Automated Quotations system (NASDAQs): NASDAQ is the second largest equity market in the USA and lists thousands of US and foreign companies. In recent years it has attracted a lot of high technology companies. The stock exchange market offers electronic trading using computers and a vast telecommunications network.

National Savings Certificates (NSC): A range of tax-free investments from the government that pay a guaranteed return. An attractive investment for tax payers, especially those paying at the higher level.

Net Asset Value (NAV): The Net Asset Value of a company is the total value of all its assets less its liabilities.

Net Yield: Net yield means the annual return on an investment after tax.

New Issue: Shares that are offered to the general public on the stock exchange for the first time.

New York Stock Exchange (NYSE): The largest and oldest stock exchange in the US, located on Wall Street in New York.

O

Opening Balance: Opening balance is the balance of an account when it is initially opened, or the balance carried over from the previous accounting period, (i.e., last accounting periods' closing balance.)

Operating Lease: An agreement whereby the leaser retains the risks and rewards associated with ownership and normally assumes responsibility for repairs, maintenance and insurance.

Operating Profit: Operating profit is the profit, which is Gross Profit — Expenses.

Order Book: It is an 'electronic book' that shows the demand for the shares of the company at various prices on a real time basis.

Overdraft: A facility granted by a bank that allows a customer holding a current account with the bank to spend more than the funds in the account. Interest is charged daily on the amount of the overdraft on that date and the overdraft is repayable at any time upon request from the bank.

Overheads: In simple the term overheads means all indirect expenses which is incurred in the business. For example: factory expenses, administrative expenses, research and development expenses, etc.

Overtrading: Overtrading is a term in financial statement analysis. It occurs when companies expand its own operations too quickly or aggressively. Overtraded companies enter a negative cycle, where increase in interest expenses negatively impact net profit leads to lesser working capital.

Offer Price: Offer price is the price at which you buy shares or units.

Open-ended: Investment fund which has no set limit either in time or money.

Option: An option is a type of financial instrument classed as derivatives because they derive their value from underlying assets. An option gives its holder the right, but not the obligation, to buy or to sell some asset on or before the option's expiration at an agreed price, the strike price. The right to buy is called a 'call option' and the right to sell is called a 'put' option.

Orphan Assets: These are the surplus assets which a life insurance company has once it has met all its liabilities to its policyholders and shareholders.

Output Tax: When the company sells its own goods or services it charges its customers VAT. This is know as output tax.

P

Paid-up Share Capital: Paid-up share capital is the total amount that shareholders of a company have paid to the company for their fully-paid shares.

Parent Undertaking: An undertaking which controls or has a dominating influence over the affairs of another undertaking.

Pareto Principle: The Pareto principle also known as the 80-20 rule. The law of the vital few and the principle of factor sacristy, states that, for many events, 80% of the effects come from 20% of the causes. Business management thinker Joseph M. Juran suggested the principle and named it after Italian economist Vilfredo Pareto, who observed that 80% of income in Italy went to 20% of the population.

Partnership: A partnership is a group of individuals who are trading together with the intention of making a profit. It usually comprise between two and twenty partners.

Payee: The person to whom money is to be, or has been paid called as payee.

Paying-in Slip: A form used for paying money into a bank account with the bank the account is held.

Personal Account: The personal account is the account which refers as any name in the world.

Personal Identification Number (PIN): A secret number issued by a bank to a customer so that the customer may use a debit or credit card in an ATM.

Petty Cash Book: A petty cash book is the book which record all the small payment in the business.

Postings: The processing of an accounting transaction, or the entering of a transaction on your accounts programme.

Pre-incorporation Profit or Loss: A profit or loss that arises immediately before a limited company is legally incorporated. Any such profit will be treated as capital profit not for distribution while, for sake of prudence; any such loss will be set against post-incorporation profits.

Preference Shares: In simple preference shares are those shares which is not the equity shares. It usually carries no voting rights, but may carry priority over common stock in the payment of dividends and upon liquidation. Preferred stock may have a convertibility feature into common stock.

Preliminary Expenses: All the costs that are incurred when a company is formed.

Prepayments: A payment for goods or services before they are received, e.g., insurance paid one year in advance and accounted for over 12 months.

Present Value: The amount that a future cash flow is worth in terms of today's money.

Prime Cost: It is the cost of direct materials plus direct labour plus direct expenses.

Private Ledger: A ledger for capital and drawing accounts.

Process Costing: A costing system that is applied when goods or services are produced in a continuous flow.

Production Cost: Prime cost plus indirect manufacturing costs.

Profit: The excess of revenues over costs in a business.

Profit and Loss Report: A report that categorizes the income and expenditure of a business over an accounting period.

Provision: An amount written off or retained by way of providing for depreciation, renewals or diminution in value of assets, or retained by way of providing for any known liability of which the amount cannot be determined with 'substantial accuracy'.

Provision for Bad Debt: An amount put by for those debts which may not be paid. It appears as an expense on the profit and loss account and is deducted from the debtors control account.

Prudence: Ensuring that profit is not shown as being too high, or that asset are shown at too high a value and that the financial statements are neutral: that is, that neither gains nor losses are understated or overstated.

Public Company: A company that can issue its shares to the general public, and for which there is no maximum number of shareholders.

Public Sector: All organizations that are not privately owned or operated.

Purchased Goodwill: The difference between the amounts paid to acquire a part or the whole of a business as a going concern and the value of the net assets owned by the business.

Purchases: Goods or services bought for the purpose of making a direct sale, e.g., Material costs such as stationary that is resold, hardware that is resold, etc.

Purchase Credit Notes: It also known as a credit note or credit memorandum (memo). It is a commercial document issued by a seller to a buyer. The seller usually issues a credit memo for the same or lower amount than the invoice, and then repays the money to the buyer or sets it off against a balance due from other transactions. They are normally issued when goods or services are faulty or when the purchase invoice was incorrect.

Purchase Discounts: Purchase discounts may be given for a variety of reasons, e.g., buying in bulk, spending large amounts, being a preferred customer.or settlement discount. It refers to just settlement discount or prompt payment discount.

Purchase Invoices: These are issued by suppliers as a request for payment in respect of the supply of goods or services.

Purchase Ledger: A purchase ledger is a system in accountancy by which a business records and monitors its creditors. It contains the individual accounts of suppliers from whom the business has made purchases on credit. The total balance outstanding should equal the balance of the creditors control account in the nominal ledger.

Purchase Payments: Payments made to suppliers in respect of invoices for the goods and/or services supplied.

Purchases Day Book: Book of original entry for credit purchases, and also called the purchases journal.

Par Value: The value of the security when it is first issued, also known as nominal value.

Passive Management: Management strategy to buy a well diversified portfolio to represent a broad-based market index without attempting to search out mispriced-securities.

Penny Shares: Shares that sells for just a few pence and are considered to be at a high risk and extremely volatile by most investors.

Placing: An arrangement whereby a new issue of shares are not offered to the general public, but instead are sold to a small number of investors, usually, institutional investors such as pension funds.

Portfolio: A portfolio is a collection of different investments that make up your total investment holding.

Preliminary Results: The results reported by a company for a full financial year before the publication of the company's annual report of accounts.

Premium: A measure of how far the share price of an investment trust is above its net asset value, expressed as a percentage of the net asset value per share.

Pre-tax Profits: A company's profits before the deduction of corporation tax.

Price-earnings Ratio (PE): The P/E ratio is the most important yardstick for assessing the relative worth of a share. It reflects the markets appraisal of the shares future prospects. A high P/E ratio suggests a company has good prospects of achieving above-average growth in the future. The P/E ratio of a company is calculated by dividing its share price by its earnings per share.

Profit and Loss Account: The profit and loss account is an important part of a company's annual accounts and gives the details of the company's trading performance for the previous financial year.

Prospectus: A document which has to be published by a company wanting to issue shares to the public in compliance with the rules and regulations of the stock exchange. It provides information on the company's business, its history, financial structure and future prospects.

Q

Quick Ratio: A ratio for calculating the liquidity position of a business. It is calculated as:

Quick Ratio = (Current Assets − Stock) ÷ Current Liabilities

Quotation: Quotation is a statement of the current market price of a service or security.

Quote: The highest bid price and the lowest offer price for a security at any particular time.

Quoted Company: A company which is listed on the stock exchange.

R

Real Accounts: Accounts in which touchable and visible generally called as real accounts. For example: property of all kinds is recorded.

Realization Concept: Only profits and gains realized at the balance sheet date should be included in the profit and loss account.

Receipt: A written acknowledgement that a specified article, sum of money, or shipment of merchandise has been received.

Receipts and Payments Account: A summary of the cash book of a non-profit-oriented organization.

Receivable: An amount awaiting receipt of payment.

Reconciliation: The process of agreeing accounting entries from one source, with entries from another source.

Reducing Balance Method: A method of calculating depreciation based on the principle that calculate annual depreciation as a percentage of the net-of-depreciation-to-date balance brought forward at the start of the period on the fixed asset.

Relevant Costs: This cost also called as avoidable cost or differential cost. A relevant cost is a cost that differs between alternatives being considered. Those costs of the future that will be affected by a decision.

Reserve Accounts: The transfer of apportioned profits to accounts for use in future years.

Residual Value: The net amount receivable when a fixed asset is put out of use by the business.

Resource Accounting: An accounting system based on normal commercial practice, including accruals and movements in cash flows.

Retention: An amount of money retained by a customer for a specified period of time after a service has been provided, to ensure that if anything should subsequently go wrong then it will be rectified.

Return on Capital Employed (RoCE): Return on Capital Employed = (Net Profit ÷ Capital Employed) × 100.

This ratio indicates how much profit in percentage terms is being earned from the money invested in the business.

Return on Owners' Equity: Net profit as a percentage of ordinary share capital plus all reserves. It abbreviated as ROOE. And the more common term in use for this return on shareholders' funds.

Returns: Goods returned to the business by a customer, or by the business to a supplier.

Returns Inwards: When the goods returned by customers called as return inward. Also known as 'sales returns'.

Returns Inwards Day Book: Book of original entry for goods returned by customers. It is also called the returns inwards journal or the sales returns day book.

Returns Outwards: When the goods returned to suppliers called as return outward. Also known as 'purchases returns'.

Returns Outwards Day Book: Book of original entry for goods returned to suppliers. It also called the returns outwards journal or the purchases returns book.

Revaluation Account: An account used to record gains and losses when assets are revalued.

Revenue: Revenue is income that a company receives from its normal business activities, usually from the sale of goods and services to customers. It is referred to as turnover.

Revenue Expenditure: Expenses needed for the day-to-day running of the business.

Revenue Reserves: The revenue reserve is that part of profit that has been not given to the shareholder but retained in the business for further growth. A balance of profits retained available to pay cash dividends including an amount voluntarily transferred from the profit and loss appropriation account.

Rights Issue: An offer to sell a new issue of shares by a company to its existing shareholders, usually at a price which is lower than the market price.

Rally: A sudden rise in the value of a share or market performance after a long fall.

Reaction: A reversal of a trend in the movement of share prices. For example, there will be a fall in the price of shares following a rally as everyone quickly tries to makes profits. Also known as a correction.

Redemption: The date a security, such as, a bond, preferred stock or mutual fund shares becomes repayable. It also called the maturity date.

Redemption Yield: The total return from a security, such as, a bond on its maturity date. It reflects both the income and capital gain/loss that it will make when it matures.

Registrar: An organization that maintains a register of the share owners and the number of shares held for a company. It also makes sure that the numbers of shares issued are not more than the number of shares authorized.

Repayment Mortgage: A mortgage where you pay-off both the capital and interest each month until you've completely repaid the loan at the end of the preagreed term.

Retail Prices Index (RPI): An inflationary indicator that measures the prices of a representative sample of household goods and services. It is a general indicator which is used to measure the rise or fall in the cost of living.

Retention Ratio: The proportion of the profits retained in a business after all the expenses usually including tax and interest are taken into account. The algorithm is retained profits divided by profits available for ordinary shareholders.

Retained Profits: The proportion of profits after tax that is not distributed as dividends but is reinvested in the company.

S

Sales: The term sales means the goods sold by the business in which it normally deals and bought with the prime intention of resale.

Sales Credit Notes: These are issued to customers in order to cancel sales invoices either in full or in part and normally issued when goods or services are faulty or when the sales invoice was incorrect.

Sales Day Book: Sales day book is the book which only the transaction relates with credit sales. It is a part of the subsidiary book.

Sales Discounts: Sales discounts may be allowed for a variety of reasons, e.g., buying in bulk, spending large amounts, being a preferred customer (trade discount) or settlement discount. In simple, it refers to just settlement discount or prompt payment discount.

Sales Invoice: Sales invoice is a document which showing the details of goods sold and the prices of those goods.

Sales Ledger: In simple it refers as the *record* of *daily sales*. It keeps track, in account order, of all invoices, credit notes and discounts sent to customers and all receipts received from customers and quickly referred to find the current status of any of the customer accounts. The total balance outstanding should equal the balance of the debtors control account in the nominal ledger.

Sales Receipts: These are made when invoices are paid-off by the recipient of the goods or services.

Sales Returns Day Book: Sales return day book is the primary record for recording credit notes.

Sensitivity Analysis: Sensitivity analysis is the analysis to see the what would be likely to happen if altering volumes and amounts. For example, a company may wish to know the financial effects of cutting its selling price. Also called 'what if' analysis.

Separate Valuation Concept: Recording and measurement rule that relates to the determination of the aggregate amount of any item. In order to determine the aggregate amount of an asset or a liability, each individual asset or liability that comprises the aggregate must be determined separately.

Settlement Discount: A CASH DISCOUNT or SETTLEMENT DISCOUNT is a percentage discount of the total invoice value that is offered to a customer to encourage that customer to pay up or settle the invoice earlier.

Shares: The division of the capital of a company into equal part and each equal part is called as share. Documents issued by a company to its owners (the shareholders) which state how many shares in the company each shareholder has bought and what percentage of the company the shareholder owns.

Share Discount: When a share is issued at a price below its par, or nominal value, known as share is issued at discount.

Share Premium: When a share is issued at a price above its par, or nominal value, known as share is issued at premium.

Simple Interest: Simple interest (I) is calculated by multiplying the amount invested sometimes called the principle, P by the length of time (T) the money is invested and the rate of interest (R) converted to a equation; that is:

$$I = (P \times R \times T)/100.$$

Single-step Income Statement: An income statement where all the revenues are shown as a single total rather than being split up into different types of revenue.

Sinking Fund: A sinking fund is a fund established by a government agency or business for the purpose of reducing debt by repaying or purchasing outstanding loans and securities held against the entity.

Sole Trader: In simple word sole trader means a single man business that trades under his or her own name. The owner is also the only party to benefit from the profits of the business, and taking money or goods out of the business is known as drawings. In simple, it is known as single man ownership business.

Source of Funds/Capital Employed: Source of funds refers as where the business collect the funds or any money invested into the business including share capital, reserves, and long-term loans. It is also called as capital employed.

Standard Cost: It is an estimated or predetermined *cost* of performing an *operation* or producing a good or *service*, under normal conditions. Standard costs are used as *target-costs* and are *developed* from *historical data analysis* and motion studies.

Standard Costing: It is a part of the technique costing. It is a control technique process that compares standard costs and standard revenues with actual costs and actual revenues in order to determine differences, generally called as variances either positive or negative.

Standard Rate: The standard rate is the rate which based on standard costing or on standard practices.

Standing Order: Standing order is an order by a customer, business or personal to their banker to pay a specified amount usually on or around a particular day of the month regularly to another account. This could be typically to a person's building society for regular payment of mortgage interest or for premiums for life in assurance.

Statement: A statement is a copy of a customer's personal account taken from the supplier's books to know the details of customers accounts.

Statement of Affairs: A statement from which the capital of the owner can be found by estimating assets and liabilities, i.e., Capital = Assets – Liabilities. It is the equivalent of the balance sheet.

Stock: The total goods or raw materials held by a business for the purpose of resale. Stock is valued in the balance sheet at the lower of cost and net realizable value. It is also known as inventory.

Stock Turnover: In simple, stock turnover means the number of times stock is sold in an accounting period. Also known as 'stock turn'.

Stock Taking: Stock taking is the process of physically verification or checking a business' stock for total quantities and value at a given point of time.

Subsidiary Undertaking: An undertaking which is controlled by another undertaking or where that other undertaking exercises a dominating influence over it.

Subsidiary Ledgers: These are ledgers where supporting or memorandum ledger accounts are kept, in addition to the main ledger. It generally consists of Purchase ledger, Sales ledger, Purchase return book, Sales return book, Bills receivable books, Bills payable books, Journal proper, etc.

Sunk Costs: Sunk sosts are retrospective (past) costs that have already been incurred and cannot be recovered. Sunk costs are sometimes contrasted with prospective costs, which are future costs that may be incurred or changed if an action is taken. In simple sunk cost a cost which has already occurred.

Super Profits: In simple super profit means, net profit less the opportunity costs of alternative earnings and alternative returns on capital invested that have been foregone.

Suspense Account: A suspense account is an account used temporarily to carry doubtful receipts and disbursements or discrepancies pending their analysis and permanent classification. It can be used as a holding account until it is decided what should be done with the value. The balance on the suspense account should ultimately be zero.

Scrip Dividend: Scrip dividend means distributes dividends in the form of shares by the company to the shareholders.

Scrip Issue: A free issue of extra shares to shareholders by a company. This arises when the share price has risen so high that they become too expensive to buy for the smaller investors and also known as a 'bonus' or 'capitalization' issue.

Secondary Market: The secondary market is a place where an investor can buy or sell existing securities. Shares will be traded in the secondary market once they have been issued in the primary market.

Securities: The term securities generally used to cover all stocks and shares.

Securities and Exchange Commission (SEC): The primary regulator for all the securities industry in the US. Its responsibility is to promote full disclosure and to protect investors against fraudulent and manipulative practices in the securities markets.

Securities and Futures Authority (SFA): The self-regulating organization (SRO) which has responsibility for regulating all firms engaged in the securities and futures sector of the financial services market. However, since December, 2001 all regulatory functions of the SFA has been absorbed into the Financial Services Authority.

Self-regulating Organization (SRO): Organizations that were set up under the Financial Services Act of 1986 to be directly responsible for policing investment businesses.

Selling Short: The practice of selling securities which are not at present owned, in the hope that they can be bought at a lower price, once the price has fallen to settle the contract.

Settlement: The payment for the securities and the delivery of the securities in return for the payment.

Shareholder: In simple the term shareholder means the owner of shares in a company. Shareholders supply what is known as the risk capital and share in the success of the company. If the company is a success and makes a profit, shareholders receive the rewards of increasing dividend income and capital gains on the price of their shares an in failure, shareholders stand to lose the whole of their investment.

Share Certificate: This is the legal proof of ownership of shares in a company. But due to increase of electronic trading and settlement systems such as crest, share certificates are gradually being phased out.

Stagging: The process of buying shares when they are initially offered to the general public and then selling them immediately to retail investors once trading has begun — with a view to making a quick profit.

Stamp Duty: Stamp duty is a tax levied on share dealings and house purchases.

Standard & Poor's Stock Index (S&P500): US performance index of a basket of 500 stocks that are considered to be widely held.

Stepped Preference Shares: Stepped preference shares are preference shares whose fixed percentage dividend will rise annually at a preset rate.

Stock Broker: A stock broker is a member of the stock exchange who buys and sells shares on your behalf for a brokerage fee.

Stock Exchange: Stock Exchange is a place where trading for stocks, shares and other securities are made.

Stock Exchange Automated Quotations (SEAQ): The SEAQ is a computerized price display and recording system for prices of gilts and of shares. SEAQ requires all competing market-makers to quote buying and selling prices along with the number of shares they are prepared to deal with at that price.

Stock Exchange Electronic Trading Service (SETS): An automated trading system that was introduced in 1997 in the London stock exchange. It matches the orders of buyers and sellers automatically, thus cutting out the need for a market-maker.

Subsidiary Company: Subsidiary company is a company that has the majority of its voting shares owned by a holding company.

Surrender Value: The cash amount received if an insurance policy is cancelled before its maturity date.

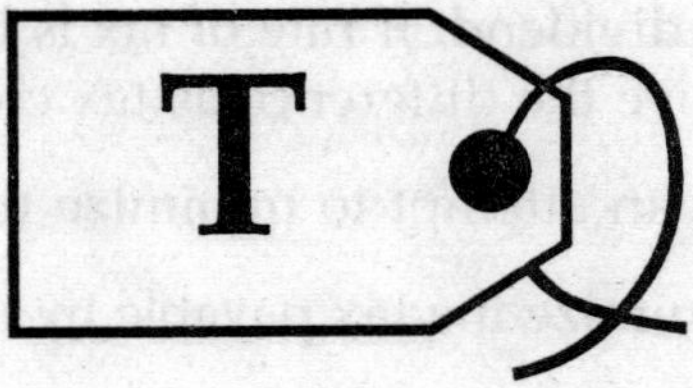

T-Account: It is the layout of accounts. T-ACCOUNT is the basis for journal entry in accounting and having certain elements. A title, a left side (debit side) and a right side (credit side).

Tangible Asset: Assets having a physical existence, such as cash, equipment, and real estate; accounts receivable are also usually considered tangible assets for accounting purposes.

Tax Code: The tax code is the number found by adding up an individual's personal allowances which is used to calculate that individual's tax liability.

Total Cost: The total cost is the cost which is incurred for the production of finished product. In general Prime Cost + Work Overheads + Administration Overheads + Selling and Distribution Overheads + Research and Development Overheads. In some case it also Fixed Cost + Variable Cost + Semi-variable Cost.

Trade Discount: A percentage reduction from the list price of goods that a business may offer to some customers at the time of huge purchase of goods.

Trading Account: Trading account is compares sales, stock used and direct expenses to find the gross profit or loss made by buying and selling.

Trading and Profit and Loss Account: Financial statements in which both gross profit or loss and net profit or loss are calculated.

Transposition Error: The transposition error is the error where the characters within a number are entered in the wrong sequence.

Trial Balance: It is a statement together with their net balances, shown as either a debit or a credit balance. It is prepare to check the arithmetically accuracy of the accounts.

True and Fair View: The expression that is used by auditors to indicate whether, in their opinion, the financial statements fairly represent the state of affairs and financial performance of a company.

Trustee: An individual or an organization which holds or manages and invests assets for the benefit of another. The trustee is legally obliged to make all trust-related decisions with the trustee's interests in mind, and may be liable for damages in the event of not doing so.

Tax Credit: Dividends payments are received in net because companies are required to deduct tax when paying out a dividend. If rate of tax is lower than the rate paid by the company, then allowed to receive the difference as tax credit.

Tax Avoidance: Tax avoidance an attempt to minimize the tax payable by legal means.

Tax Evasion: An attempt to minimize the tax payable by illegal means, e.g., by reporting inaccurately.

Tax Year: The tax year begins on April 6 and ends on April 5 the following year.

Tender Offer: Tender offer means it a way of raising capital by inviting investors to make bids for the price they are willing to pay for the shares.

Term Insurance: In life insurance, the insurance policy set up for a specified number of years. This specified number of year generally called as a term.

Tied Agent: A tied agent is a financial salesman who can only offer to sell the financial products of one company, rather than looking at the whole market for products that best suit you.

Total Return: The total return on an investment is the combination of both the income return and any capital gain or loss.

Tracker Fund: An index tracker fund is a collective investment vehicle that is designed to follow the performance of a particular index. The simplest way to track an index would be to buy every share in the index at exactly its weight in the index and rebalance as companies are deleted from or added to the index.

U

Undertrading: Undertrading is usually caused by management's poor use of investment money and their general lack of ingenuity, skill or aggressiveness.

Unpresented Cheques: Cheques paid out which are passing through the bank clearing system, but have not yet been presented to the bank where the account is maintained.

Unquoted Investments: Unquoted investment means an investment not dealt in on a recognized stock exchange. It also known as unlisted investments.

Underperformance: It generally called as poor performance. An investment that does not grow as fast as other similar investments.

Underwriter: An investor or institution who agrees to take up the unsubscribed shares should there prove to be little demand by investors, when a new issue of shares or securities takes place. Underwriters will receive a handsome fee for taking on this risk.

Unit Trust: A unit trust is a mutual fund or collective investment that pools investors' cash and invests it on their behalf. It is the role of the unit trust manager to make sure that the money is invested properly and delivers the best return for the investors.

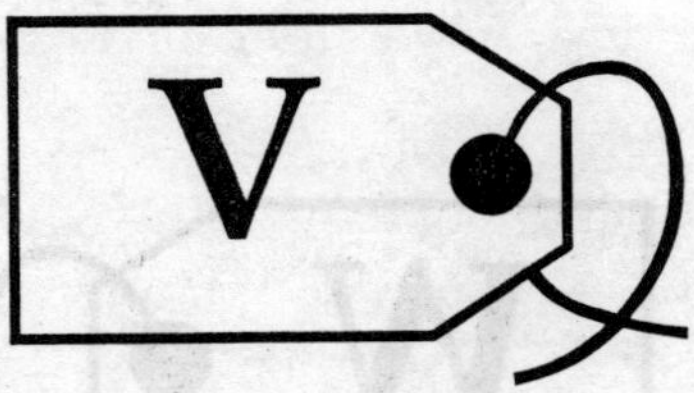

Valuation: It is a formal assessment of the worth of property, goods, etc.

Value-added Tax (VAT): VAT is a tax imposed by the government on certain goods/ services supplied. It is applied to all VAT registered businesses for a net sale or purchase amount.

Variable Costs: Variable cost is the cost which is varies as per the change of output. It generally change in total but constant in per unit. In simple change of expenses as to changes in the level of activity.

Variance: In simple it is nothing, it is only the difference between budget or standard and actual. It also describes the difference between the opening and closing balance of an account.

Variance Analysis: A means of assessing the difference between a predetermined cost/ income and the actual cost/income.

VAT Cash Accounting: A special arrangement for accounting for VAT, that must be agreed with the Customs and Excise department, by which VAT is charged on amounts actually received net of amounts paid, rather than on the invoices for those amounts.

VAT Invoice: An invoice issued by a supplier registered for VAT showing the supplier's VAT registration number, the date of issue and the tax point.

Venture Capital (VC): Funds that are made available to small young companies who have high growth potential. Managerial and technical advisors may also provide their services in this type of investment.

Volatility: The relative rate at which the price of a security rises and falls over time. This is found by calculating the annualized standard deviation of daily changes in price.

Volume: The number of bonds, shares and securities that are traded on the stock exchange for a given period.

Voting Right: Ownership of shares usually gives the shareholder the right to vote in election for directors of the company and other corporate policy matters. One share means one vote.

Wall Street: The name of the famous street on which the New York stock exchange and other major financial institutions are located.

Warrants: Warrants are risky investments which give the holder the right to buy a given number of shares in a company at a fixed price at some future date usually several years ahead. A warrant is a right and not an obligation to buy.

Whole-of-life Insurance: An insurance policy that covers your entire life. It is not like term insurance, which only lasts for a set period.

'What If': Altering volumes and amounts so as to see what would be likely to happen if they were changed. For example, a company may wish to know the financial effects of cutting its selling price by £1 a unit. Also called sensitivity analysis.

Winding-up: It is also called as liquidation. The end of a company by selling off its assets to pay-off creditors and distributing the remaining funds to its shareholders.

With-profits Policies: Investment-based insurance policies are investments whose returns are in the form of bonuses which depend on profits made by insurers. There are many factors which influence the level of bonuses, including the return the insurer gets on investing premiums, cost levels, claims experience, whether there are shareholders who receive part of the profits, and the extent to which the company tries to smooth bonus levels from one year to the next.

Work Certified: Work certified is one type of certified valuation by an architect or an engineer on a contract costing to evaluate the value of work-in-progress.

Work-in-progress (W.I.P): The value of partly finished of work at the end of an accounting period.

Working Capital: The working capital is the capital which is required to maintain the day-to-day operation of the business. In an accounting term it is the excess of current assets over the current liabilities. It also net current assets.

Write-off: It is a term which is generally used to cancel a bad debt or obsolete asset from the accounts or, to consider a transaction as a loss or set off a loss against revenues or, to charge a specified amount against gross profits as depreciation of an asset.

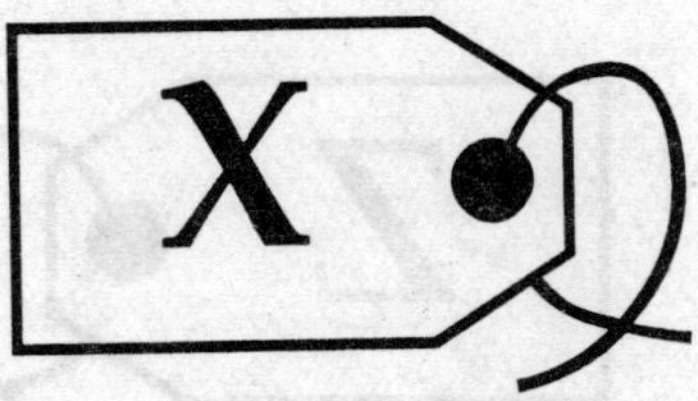

XD: It short for exdividend. It reflects a share price where the most recent dividend has been paid-out but anyone buying the share will not get this benefit.

Yield: The term yield describes the amount in cash that returns to the owners of a security. In simply it is the return on an investment expressed as a percentage.

Yield Curve: The yield curve is the relation between the interest rate or cost of borrowing and the time to maturity of the debt for a given borrower in a given currency.

Yield to Maturity: The Yield to maturity (YTM) or redemption yield of a bond or other fixed-interest security, such as gilts, is the internal rate of return (IRR) earned by an investor who buys the bond today at the market price, assuming that the bond will be held until maturity. All coupon and principal payments will be made on schedule. It is actually an estimation of future return.

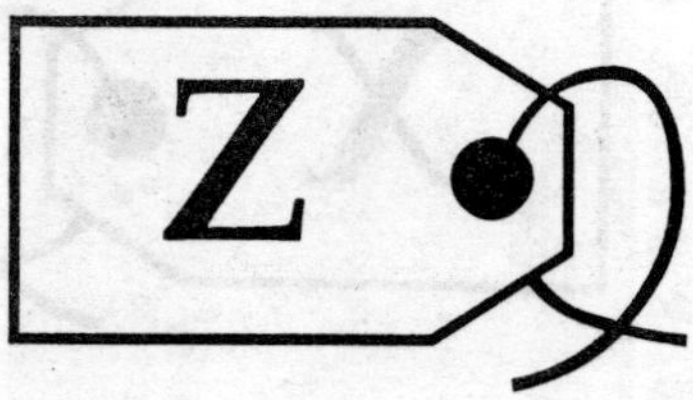

Zero-rated: Zero-rated on which the buyer pays no VAT although the seller can claim back any tax he/she has paid. It include some food items, newspapers, magazines and books, medicine and children's clothing.

Zero-rated Business: A business that only supplies zero-rated goods and services. It does not charge VAT to its customers but it receives a refund of VAT on goods and services it purchases.

Zero Coupon Bonds: A zero-coupon bond also called a discount bond or deep discount **bond.** It is a bond bought at a price lower than its face value but at the time of maturity it repaid at face value. It does not make periodic interest payments and the investors earn return from the compounded interest all paid at maturity plus the difference between the discounted price of the bond and its par or redemption value.

Zero Dividend Preference Share ('zeros'): Zeros are capital shares in a split-capital investment trust. They do not receive any dividend income but get part of the capital growth of the assets held by the trust when the trust is wound up.

Zero-based Budgeting: Zero-based budgeting is a technique of planning and decision-making which reverses the working process of traditional budgeting. In traditional incremental budgeting, departmental managers justify only increases over the previous year budget and what has been already spent is automatically sanctioned. Zero-based budgeting requires the budget request be justified in complete detail by each division manager starting from the zero-base.

Zero Balance Account: A zero balance account in which a balance of zero is maintained by automatically transferring funds from a master account in an amount only large enough to cover checks presented.

End

2 Glossary: Accounting Term

A

Above the Line: This term can be applied to many aspects of accounting. It means transactions, assets, etc., that are associated with the everyday running of a business.

Accounting Cycle: Accounting cycle means covering everything from opening the books at the start of the year to closing them at the end. In other words, everything you need to do in one accounting year accounting wise.

Accounting Equation: The term accounting equation generally refers as *assets = liability + equity* .

Accounts Payable: An account in the *nominal* ledger which contains the overall balance of the purchase ledger.

Accounts Payable Ledger: A subsidiary ledger which holds the accounts of a business' suppliers. A single control account is held in the *nominal* ledger which shows the total balance of all the accounts in the purchase ledger.

Accounts Receivable: In simple accounts receivable means an account in the *nominal* ledger which contains the overall balance of the sales ledger.

Accounts Receivable Ledger: A subsidiary ledger which holds the accounts of a business' customers. A single control account is held in the *nominal* ledger which shows the total balance of all the accounts in the sales ledger.

Accruals: If during the course of a business certain charges are incurred but no invoice is received then these charges are referred to as accruals. A typical example is interest payable on a loan where you have not yet received a bank statement. These items should still be included in the profit and loss account. Accruals can also apply to the income side.

Accumulated Depreciation Account: This is an account held in the *nominal* ledger which holds the depreciation of a fixed asset until the end of the asset's useful life. It is credited each year with that year's depreciation, hence the balance increases, (i.e., accumulates), over a period of time. Each fixed asset will have its own accumulated depreciation account.

Amortization: The depreciation of an intangible asset over a fixed period of time. Example: if a loan of 12,000 is amortized over one year with no interest, the monthly payments would be 1,000 a month.

Appropriation Account: An account in the *nominal* ledger which shows how the net profits of a business (usually a partnership, limited company or corporation) have been used.

At Cost: The 'at cost' price usually refers to the price originally paid for something, as opposed to, say, the retail price.

Audit: The process of checking every entry in a set of books to make sure they agree with the original paperwork, (e.g., checking a journal's entries against the original purchase and sales invoices).

Audit Trail: A list of transactions in the order they occurred.

Bad Debts Account: An account in the nominal ledger to record the value of unrecoverable debts from customers.

Bad Debts Reserve Account: An account used to record an estimate of bad debts for the year (usually as a percentage of sales). This cannot be deducted as an expense against tax liability.

Balancing Charge: When a fixed asset is sold or disposed of, any loss or gain on the asset can be reclaimed against any profits for income tax purposes. This is called a balancing charge.

Bankrupt: If an individual or unincorporated company has greater liabilities than it has assets, the person or business can petition for, or be declared by its creditors, bankrupt. In the case of a limited company or corporation in the same position, the term used is *insolvent*.

Below the Line: This term is applied to items within a business which would not normally be associated with the everyday running of a business.

Bill: A term typically used to describe a purchase invoice.

Burn Rate: The rate at which a company spends its money. Example: if a company had cash reserves of $120m and it was currently spending $10m a month, then you could say that at the current 'burn rate' the company will run out of cash in one year.

C

CAGR: (Compound Annual Growth Rate) The year- on- year growth rate required to show the change in value of an investment from its initial value to its final value. If a $1 investment was worth $1.52 over three years, the CAGR would be 15% [(1× 1.15) ×1.15 ×1.15]

Called-up Share Capital: The value of unpaid but issued shares which a company has requested payment for.

Capital Account: A term usually applied to the owner's equity in the business.

Capital Employed (CE): Gross CE=Total assets, **Net** CE = Fixed assets plus (current assets less current liabilities).

Capital Gains Tax: When a fixed asset is sold at a profit, the profit may be liable to a tax called Capital Gains Tax.

Cash Accounting: This term describes an accounting method whereby only invoices and bills which have been paid are accounted for. However, for most types of business in UK, as far as the inland revenue are concerned as soon as you issue an invoice (paid or not), it is treated as revenue and must be accounted for. An exception is VAT: Customs and Excise normally, require you to account for VAT on an accrual basis, however there is an option called 'Cash Accounting' whereby only paid items are included as far as VAT is concerned.

Cash Flow: A report which shows the flow of money in and out of the business over a period of time.

Charge Back: Charge back refers to a credit card order which has been processed and is subsequently cancelled by the cardholder contacting the credit card company directly. This results in the amount being 'charged back' to the seller.

Chart of Accounts: A list of all the accounts held in the *nominal* ledger.

CIF (Cost, Insurance, Freight [CIF]): A contract for the sale of goods where the seller agrees to supply the goods, pay the insurance, and pay the freight charges until the goods reach the destination (usually a port — rather than the actual buyers address). After that point, the responsibility for the goods passes to the buyer.

Circulating Assets: The opposite to *fixed assets*. Circulating assets describe those assets that turn from cash to goods and back again.

Closing the Books: A term used to describe the journal entries necessary to close the sales and expense accounts of a business at year end by posting their balances to the profit and loss account, and ultimately to close the profit and loss account too by posting its balance to a capital or other account.

Compensating Error: A double-entry term applied to a mistake which has cancelled out another mistake.

Compound Interest: Apply interest on the capital plus all interest accrued to date., e.g, A/c loan with an annually applied rate of 10% for 1,000 over two years would yield a gross total of 1,210 at the end of the period (year one interest = 100, year two interest = 110). The same loan with *simple interest* applied would yield 1,200 (interest on both years is 100 per year).

Control Account: An account held in a ledger which summarizes the balance of all the accounts in the same or another ledger. Typically each subsidiary ledger will have a control account which will be mirrored by another control account in the *nominal* ledger.

Cook the Books: Cook the books generally refers as the falsify a set of accounts.

Cost Accounting: An area of *management accounting* which deals with the costs of a business in terms of enabling the management to manage the business more effectively.

Cost-based Pricing: Where a company bases its pricing policy solely on the costs of manufacturing rather than current market conditions.

Cost-benefit: Calculating not only the financial costs of a project, but also the cost of the effects it will have from a social point of view. This is not easy to do since it requires valuations of intangible items like the cost of job losses or the effects on the environment.

Cost Centre: Splitting up expenses by departmentwise rather than having one account to handle all power costs for a company, a power account would be opened for each department.

Cost of Finished Goods: The value of newly manufactured goods shown in a business' manufacturing account. The valuation is based on the opening raw materials balance, less direct costs involved in manufacturing, less the closing raw materials balance, and less any other overheads. This balance is subsequently transferred to the trading account.

Cost of Goods Sold (COGS): A formula for working out the direct costs of stock sold over a particular period. The result represents the gross profit. The formula is: Opening Stock + Purchases – Closing Stock.

Cost of Sales: A formula for working out the direct costs of sales (including stock) over a particular period. The result represents the gross profit. The formula is: Opening Stock + Purchases + Direct Expenses – Closing Stock.

Creative Accounting: Creative accounting means making companies figures appear more or less appealing to shareholders, etc. An example is 'branding' where the 'value' of a brand name is added to intangible assets which increases shareholders funds.

Credit: A column in a journal or ledger to record the 'From' side of a transaction.

Creditors: A list of suppliers to whom the business owes money.

Current Cost Accounting: The valuing of assets, stock, raw materials, etc., at current market value as opposed to its *historical* cost.

Days Sales Outstanding (DSO): Days sales outstanding means how long on average it takes a company to collect the money owed to it.

Debtors: A list of customers who owe money to the business.

Debtors (Control Account): An account in the *nominal* ledger which contains the overall balance of the sales ledger.

Deferred Expenditure: Deferred expenditure refers as the expenditure which is incurred within the current accounting period but the benefit goes to more than that accounting period.

Double-entry Bookkeeping: A system which accounts for every aspect of a transaction — where it came from and where it went to. This *from* and *to* aspect of a transaction (called crediting and debiting) is what the term double-entry means. Modern double-entry was first mentioned by G Cotrugli, then expanded upon by L Paccioli in the 15th century.

Drawings: The money taken out of a business by its owner(s) for personal use.

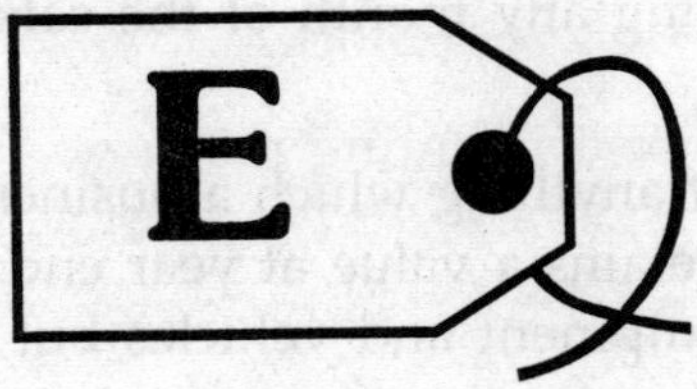

EBIT: Earnings before interest and tax, i.e., profit before any interest or taxes have been deducted.

EBITA: Earnings before interest, tax and amortization, i.e., profit before any interest, taxes or *amortization* have been deducted.

EBITDA: Earnings before interest, tax, depreciation and amortization, i.e., profit before any interest, taxes, *depreciation* or *amortization* have been deducted.

Entry: Part of a transaction recorded in a journal or posted to a ledger.

Error of Original Entry: A double-entry term which means that a transaction has been entered with the wrong amount.

Error of Principle: A double-entry term which means that one or both sides of a double-entry has been posted to the wrong account. Example: Petrol expense posted to fixtures and fittings.

Expenses: Goods or services purchased directly for the running of the business. This does not include goods bought for resale or any items of a capital nature.

F

Fiscal Year: The term used for a business' accounting year. The period is usually twelve months which can begin during any month of the calendar year, i.e., 1st April to 31st March.

Fixed Assets: These consist of anything which a business owns or buys for use within the business and which still retains a value at year end. They usually consist of major items like land, buildings, equipment and vehicles but can include smaller items like tools.

Fixtures and Fittings: This is a class of fixed asset which includes office furniture, filing cabinets, display cases, warehouse shelving and the like.

Flash Earnings: A news release issued by a company that shows its latest quarterly results.

Flow of Funds: This is a report which shows how a balance sheet has changed from one period to the next.

FOB: It is stand for Free On Board. It generally forms part of an export contract where the seller pays all the costs and insurance of sending the goods to the port of shipment. After that, the buyer then takes full responsibility. If the goods are to travel by train, it's called FOR, i.e., Free On Rail.

G

Gearing: The comparison of a company's long-term fixed interest loans compared to its assets. In general two different methods are used:

1. Balance sheet gearing is calculated by dividing long-term loans with the equity or proprietor's networth.
2. Profit and loss gearing: Fixed interest payments for the period divided by the profit for the period.

Goodwill: This is an extra value placed on a business if the owner of a business decides it is worth more than the value of its assets. It is usually included where the business is to be sold as a going concern.

Gross Loss: The balance of the trading account assuming it has a debit balance.

Gross Margin: The difference between the selling price of a product or service and the cost of that product or service often shown as a percentage. For example: if a product sold for 100 and cost 60 to buy or manufacture, the gross margin would be 40%. Gross margin can also be expressed on the total revenue and costs of producing that revenue as well as on an item by item basis.

Gross Profit: The balance of the trading account assuming it has a credit balance.

Growth and Acquisition (G&A): Describes the way a company can grow. Growth means expanding through its normal operations, acquisition means growth through buying up other companies.

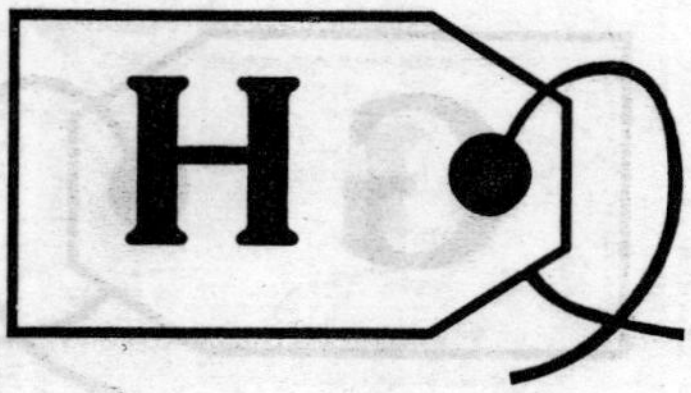

Historical Cost: Assets, stock, raw materials, etc., can be valued at what they originally cost or what they would cost to replace at today's prices.

Income: Money received by a business from its commercial activities.

Inland Revenue: The government department usually responsible for collecting your tax generally called as inland revenue.

Insolvent: A company is insolvent if it has insufficient funds to pay its debts. If a company's liabilities are greater than its assets and it continues to trade, it is not only insolvent, it is also called as illegally operating.

Intangible Assets: Assets of a non-physical or financial nature. An asset such as a loan or an endowment policy is good examples.

Inventory: A subsidiary ledger which is usually used to record the details of individual items of stock. Inventories can also be used to hold the details of other assets of a business.

Invoice: A term describing an original document either issued by a business for the sale of goods on credit, i.e., sales invoice or received by the business for goods bought, i.e., purchase invoice.

Journal(s): A book or set of books where your transactions are first entered.

Journal Entries: A term used to describe the transactions recorded in a journal.

Journal Proper: A term used to describe the main or general journal where other journals specific to subsidiary ledgers are also used.

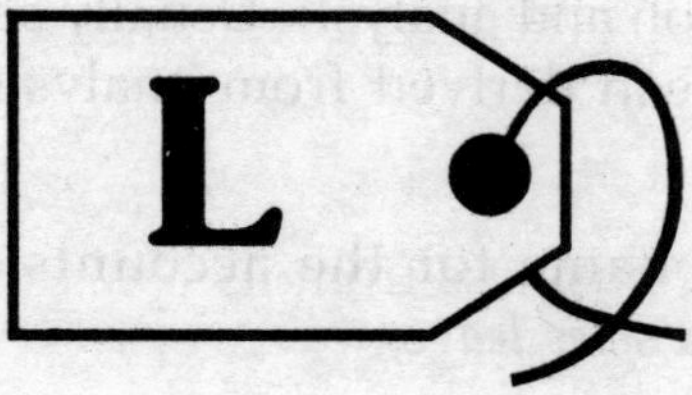

Landed Costs: The total costs involved when importing goods. They include buying, shipping, insuring and associated taxes.

Long-term Liabilities: The long-term liabilities are those liabilities which takes more than one year for repay it.

M

Management Accounting: Accounts and reports are tailor-made for the use of the managers and directors of a business as opposed to financial accounts which are prepared for the inland revenue and any other parties not directly connected with the business.

Manufacturing Account: An account used to show what it cost to produce the finished goods made by a manufacturing business.

Matching Principle: A method of analyzing the sales and expenses which make-up those sales to a particular period.

MD&A: Management discussion and analysis. Usually seen in a financial report and the information disclosed have been derived from analysis and discussions held by the management.

Memorandum Accounts: A name for the accounts held in a subsidiary ledger. For example, the accounts in a *sales ledger.*

Minority Interest: A minority interest represents a minority of shares not held by the holding company of a subsidiary. It means that the subsidiary is not wholly-owned by the holding company. The minority shareholdings are shown in the holding company accounts as *long-term liabilities.*

Multiple-step Income Statement: An income statement which has had its revenue section split up into subsections in order to give a more detailed view of its sales operations. Example: a company sells services and goods. The statement could show revenue from services and associated costs of those revenues at the start of the revenue section, then show goods sold and cost of goods sold underneath.

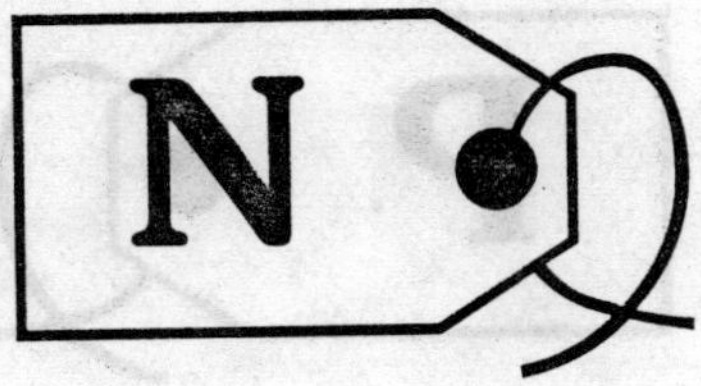

Narrative: A comment appended to an entry in a journal and it can be used to describe the nature of the transaction.

Net of Tax: The price less any tax. For example, if you sold some goods for $12 inclusive of $2 sales tax, then the 'net of tax' price would be $10.

Net Profit: The value of sales less expenses assuming that the sales are greater.

Normalize: This term can be applied to many aspects of accounting. It means to average or smooth out a set of figures so they are more consistent with the general trend of the business.

Opening the Books: Every time a business closes the books for a year, it opens a new set. The new set of books will be empty; therefore the balances from the last balance sheet must be copied into them so that the business is ready to start the new year.

Original Book of Entry: A book which contains the details of the day-to- day transactions of a business.

P

Pareto Optimum: An economic theory by Vilfredo Pareto. It states that the optimum allocation of a society's resources will not happen whilst at least one person thinks he is better off and where others perceive themselves to be no worse.

Pay on Delivery: The buyer pays the cost of the goods (to the carrier) on receipt of them.

Periodic Inventory: A periodic inventory is one whose balance is updated on a periodic basis, i.e., every week/month/year.

PE Ratio: An equation which gives you a very rough estimate as to how much confidence there is in a company's shares. The equation is: current share price multiplied by earnings and divided by the number of shares.

Perpetual Inventory: A Perpetual inventory is one whose balance is updated after each and every transaction.

Point of Sale (PoS): The place where a sale of goods takes place, e.g., a shop counter.

Post-closing Trial Balance: This is a trial balance prepared after the balance sheet has been drawn up, and only includes balance sheet accounts.

Posting: The copying of entries from the journals to the ledgers.

Pre-payments: One or more accounts set up to account for money paid in advance, i.e., insurance, where part of the premium applies to the current financial year, and the remainder to the following year.

Price Change Accounting: Accounting for the value of assets, stock, raw materials, etc., by their current market value instead of the more traditional historic *cost*.

Profit Margin: The percentage difference between the costs of a product and the price you sell it for, e.g., if a product costs you $10 to buy and you sell it for $20, then you have a 100% profit margin. This is also known as 'mark-up'.

Proforma Accounts (Proforma Financial Statements): A set of accounts prepared before the accounts have been officially audited. Often done for internal purposes or to brief shareholders or the press.

Proforma Invoice: An invoice sent that requires payment before any goods or services have been dispatched.

Provisions: One or more accounts set up to account for expected future payments.

Raw Materials: It refers to the materials bought by a manufacturing business in order to manufacture its products.

Realization Principle: The principle whereby the value of an asset can only be determined when it is sold or otherwise disposed of its 'real' value.

Reconciling: The procedure of checking entries made in a business' books with those on a statement sent by a third person.

Reserve Accounts: Reserve accounts are usually set up to make a balance sheet clearer by reserving or apportioning some of a business' capital against future purchases or liabilities.

Retail: A term usually applied to a shop which ressells other people's goods. This type of business will require a trading account as well as a profit and loss account.

Retained Earnings: This is the amount of money held in a business after its owner(s) have taken their share of the profits.

Retainer: A sum of money paid in order to ensure a person or company is available when required.

Retention Ratio: The proportion of the profits retained in a business after all the expenses usually including tax and interest are taken into account.

S

Sales Ledger: A subsidiary ledger which holds the accounts of a business' customers. A control account is held in the *nominal* ledger usually called a debtors' control account which shows the total balance of all the accounts in the sales ledger.

Self-balancing Ledgers: A system which makes use of control accounts so that each ledger will balance on its own. A control account in a subsidiary ledger will be mirrored with a control account in the *nominal* ledger.

Shares: The total capital of the company is divided into equal parts, each equal part is called share. The person who purchase the share is called as the shareholder.

Shares Issued: The number of shares a company has issued to shareholders.

Sinking Fund: An account set up to reduce another account to zero overtime using the principles of amortization or straight-line depreciation. Once the sinking fund reaches the same value as the other account, both can be removed from the balance sheet.

Source Document: An original invoice, bill or receipt to which journal entries refer.

Stock: The full value of the share called as the stock.

Stock Control Account: An account held in the *nominal* ledger which holds the value of all the stock held in the inventory subsidiary ledger.

Stock Taking: Stock taking means physically checking a business' stock for total quantities and value.

Stock Valuation: Valuing a stock of goods bought for manufacturing or resale.

Subordinated Debt: If a company is liquidated the secured creditors are paid first. If any money is left, the unsecured creditors are then paid. The amount of money owed to the unsecured creditors is termed the 'subordinated debt' of the company.

Suspense Account: A temporary account used to force a trial balance-to-balance if there is only a small discrepancy. A typical example would be a small error in petty cash. In this case a transfer would be made to a suspense account to balance the cash account.

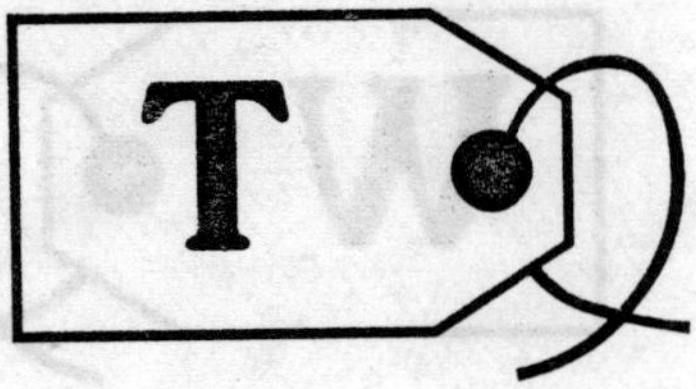

T-account: A particular method of displaying an account where the debits and associated information are shown on the left, and credits and associated information on the right.

Tangible Assets: In simple tangible assets means the physical existence of the assets. Examples include buildings, motor vehicles, plant and equipment, fixtures and fittings.

Three Column Cash Book: A journal which deals with the day-to-day cash and bank transactions of a business. The side of a transaction which relates directly to the cash or bank account is usually balanced within the journal and used as a part of the nominal ledger when compiling a balance sheet.

Trading Account: An account which shows the gross profit or loss of a manufacturing or retail business, i.e., sales less the cost of sales.

Trial Balance: A trial balance is a statement showing all the balance of ledger accounts. It is prepared to check the arithmetical accuracy of the accounts.

Turnover: In simple the term turnover means sales. The income of a business over a period of time usually a year.

Undeposited Funds Account: An account used to show the current total of money received. The 'funds' can include money, cheques, credit card payments, banker's drafts, etc. This type of account is also commonly referred to as a 'cash in hand' account.

W

Wages: Payments made to the employees of a business for their work on behalf of the business. These are classed as expense items and must not be confused with 'drawings' taken by sole-proprietors and partnerships.

Work-in-progress: The value of partly finished, (i.e., partly manufactured) goods.

Z

Zero Based Account (ZBA): Usually applied to a personal account where the balance is kept as close to zero as possible by transferring money between that account and, say, a deposit account.

Zero Based Budget (ZBB): Starting a budget at zero and justifying every cost that increases that budget.

End

3 Glossary: Derivative Terms

A

Actuals: Actuals are the financial instruments that exist in one of the four main asset classes: interest rates, foreign exchange, equities or commodities. Typically, derivatives are used to hedge actual exposure or to take positions in actual markets.

All or Nothings: An option whose payout is fixed at the inception of the option contract and for which the payout is only made if the strike price is in-the-money at expiry. If the strike price is out-of-the-money at expiry, there is no payout made to the option holder.

American Style Option: An option that can be exercised at any time from inception. Early exercise of American options may be warranted by arbitrage and exercise in most cases.

Accreting Swap: An exchange of interest rate payments at regular intervals based upon pre-set indices and notional amounts in which the notional amounts decrease overtime.

Arbitrage: The act of taking advantage of differences in price between markets. For example, if a stock is quoted on two different equity markets, there is the possibility of arbitrage if the quoted price in one market differs from the quoted price in the other. The term has been extended to refer to speculators who take positions on the correlation between two different types of instrument, assuming stability to the correlation patterns.

Asset-liability Management: Closing out exposure to fluctuations in interest rates by matching the timing of cash flows associated with assets and liabilities. This is a technique commonly used by financial institutions and large corporations.

At-the-Market: A type of financial transaction in which the order to buy or sell is executed at the current prevailing market price.

At-the-money Spot: An option whose strike price is equal to the current, prevailing price in the underlying cash spot market.

At-the-money Forward: An option whose strike price is equal to the current, prevailing price in the underlying forward market.

Average Rate Options: An option whose payout at expiry is determined by the difference between its strike and a calculated average market rate where the period, frequency and source of observation for the calculation of the average market rate are specified at the inception of the contract.

Average Strike Options: An option, whose payout at expiry is determined by the difference between the prevailing cash spot rate at expiry and its strike, deemed to be equal to a calculated average market rate where the period, frequency and source of observation for the calculation of the average market rate are specified at the inception of the contract.

B

Backwardation: A term often used in commodities or futures markets to refer to markets where short-dated contracts trade at a higher price than long-dated contracts. Plotting the prices of contracts against time, with time on the x-axis, shows the commodity price curve as sloping downwards as time increases.

Barrier Options: An option contract for which the maturity, strike price and underlying are specified at inception in addition to a trigger price. The trigger price determines whether or not the option actually exists. In the case of a knock-in option, the barrier option does not exist until the trigger is touched. For a knock-out option, the option exists until the trigger is touched.

Basis: The difference in price or yield between two different indices.

Benchmarking: A benchmark is a reference point. Benchmarking in financial risk management refers to the practice of comparing the performance of an individual instrument, a portfolio or an approach to risk management to a predetermined alternative approach.

Blackscholes: A closed-form solution (i.e., an equation) for valuing plain vanilla options developed by Fischer Black and Myron Scholes in 1973 for which they shared the Nobel Prize in Economics.

Call Option: A call option is a financial contract giving the owner the right but not the obligation to buy a pre-set amount of the underlying financial instrument at a pre-set price with a pre-set maturity date.

Cap: A cap is a financial contract giving the owner the right but not the obligation to borrow a pre-set amount of money at a pre-set interest rate with a pre-set maturity date.

Cash Settlement: Some derivative contracts are settled at maturity or before maturity at closeout by an exchange of cash from the party who is out-of-the-money to the party who is in-the-money.

Chooser Option: An option that gives the buyer the right at the choice date (before the option's expiry) to choose if the option is to be a call or a put.

Collar: A combination of options in which the holder of the contract has bought one out-of-the-money option call (or put) and sold one (or more) out-of-the-money puts (or calls). Doing this locks in the minimum and maximum rates that the collar owner will use to transact in the underlying at expiry.

Commodity Swap: A contract in which counter parties agree to exchange payments related to indices, at least one of which is a commodity index.

Contango: A term often used in commodities or futures markets to refer to markets where shorter-dated contracts trade at a lower price than longer-dated contracts. Plotting the prices of contracts against time, with time on the x-axis, shows the commodity price curve as sloping upwards as time increases.

Convexity: A financial instrument is said to be convex (or to possess convexity) if the financial instrument's price increases (decreases) faster (slower) than corresponding changes in the underlying price.

Correlation: Correlation is a statistical measure describing the extent to which prices on different instruments move together overtime. It can be positive or negative. Instruments that move together in the same direction to the same extent have highly positive correlations. Instruments that move together in opposite direction to the same extent have highly negative correlations. Correlation between instruments is not stable.

Covered Call Option Writing: A technique used by investors to help fund their underlying positions, typically used in the equity markets. An individual who sells a call is said to "write" the call. If this individual sells a call on a notional amount of the underlying that he has in his inventory, then the written call is said to be "covered" (by his inventory of the underlying).

Credit Risk: Credit risk is the risk of loss from counterparty in default or from a pejorative change in the credit status of a counterparty that causes the value of their obligations to decrease.

Currency Swap: An exchange of interest rate payments in different currencies on a pre-set notional amount and in reference to predetermined interest rate indices in which the notional amounts are exchanged at inception of the contract and then re-exchanged at the termination of the contract at pre-set exchange rates.

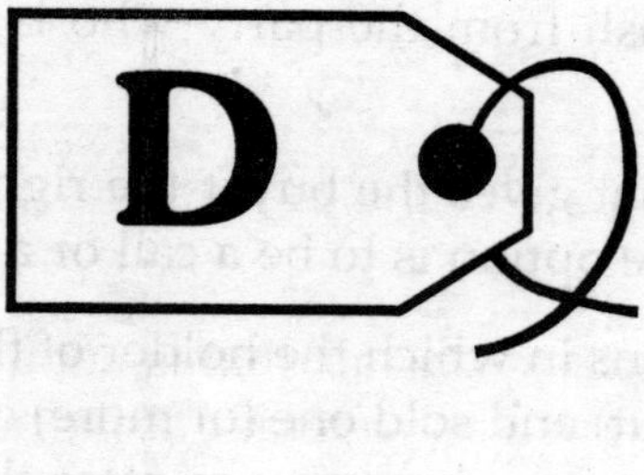

Delta: The sensitivity of the change in the financial instrument's price to changes in the price of the underlying cash index.

Documentation Risk: The risk of loss due to an inadequacy or other unforeseen aspect of the legal documentation behind the financial contract.

Duration: A weighted average of the cash flows for a fixed income instrument, expressed in terms of time.

Embedded Derivatives: Derivative contracts that exist as part of securities.

Equity Swap: A contract in which counter-parties agree to exchange payments related to indices, at least one of which is an equity index.

European Style Option: An option that can be exercised only at expiry date of the contract.

Exchange Traded Contracts: Financial instruments listed on exchanges such as the Chicago Board of Trade.

Exercise Price: The exercise price is the price at which a call's (put's) buyer can buy (or sell) the underlying instrument.

Exotic Derivatives: Any derivative contract that is not a plain vanilla contract. Examples include barrier options, average rate and average strike options, lookback options, chooser options, etc.

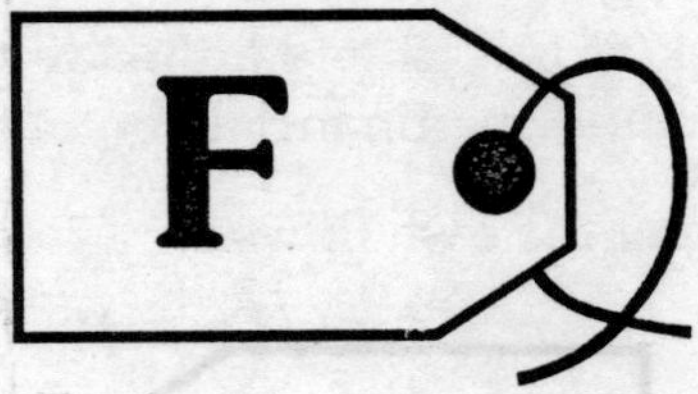

Floor: A floor is a financial contract giving the owner the right but not the obligation to lend a pre-set amount of money at a pre-set interest rate with a pre-set maturity date.

Forward Contracts: An over-the-counter obligation to buy or sell a financial instrument or to make a payment at some point in the future, the details of which were settled privately between the two counter parties. Forward contracts generally are arranged to have zero mark-to-market value at inception, although they may be off-market. Examples include forward foreign exchange contracts in which one party is obligated to buy foreign exchange from another party at a fixed rate for delivery on a pre-set date.

Forward or Delayed Start Swap: Any swap contract with a start that is later than the standard terms. This means that calculation of the cash flows does not begin straightaway but at some predetermined start date.

Forward Rate Agreements (FRAs): A forward rate agreement is a cash-settled obligation on interest rates for a pre-set period on a pre-set interest rate index with a forward start date. An interest rate swap is a strip of FRAs.

Futures Contracts: An exchange-traded obligation to buy or sell a financial instrument or to make a payment at one of the exchange's fixed delivery dates, the details of which are transparent publicly on the trading floor and for which contract settlement takes place through the exchange's clearing house.

G

Gamma: Gamma is the degree of curvature in the financial contract's price curve with respect to its underlying price. It is the rate of change of the delta with respect to changes in the underlying price. Positive gamma is favourable. Negative gamma is damaging in a sufficiently volatile market.

H

Hedge: A transaction that offsets an exposure to fluctuations in financial prices of some other contract or business risk. It may consist of cash instruments or derivatives.

Historical Volatility: A measure of the actual volatility observed in the marketplace.

Hybrid Security: Any security that includes more than one component. For example, a hybrid security might be a fixed income note that includes a foreign exchange option or a commodity price option.

Implied Volatility: Option pricing models rely upon an assumption of future volatility as well as the spot price, interest rates, the expiry date, the delivery date, the strike, etc. If we are given simultaneously all of the parameters necessary for determining the option price except for volatility and the option price in the marketplace, we can back out mathematically the volatility corresponding to that price and those parameters. This is the implied volatility.

In-the-money Spot: An option with positive intrinsic value with respect to the prevailing market spot rate. If the option were to mature immediately, the optionholder would exercise it in order to capture its economic value. For a call price to have intrinsic value, the strike must be less than the spot price. For a put price to have intrinsic value, the strike must be greater than the spot price.

In-the-money Forward: An option with positive intrinsic value with respect to the prevailing market forward rate. If the option were to mature immediately, the optionholder would exercise it in order to capture its economic value. For a call price to have intrinsic value, the strike must be less than the spot price. For a put price to have intrinsic value, the strike must be greater than the spot price.

Index Amortizing Swaps: An interest rate swap in which the notional amount for the purposes of calculating cash flows decreases over the life of the contract in a pre-specified manner.

Interest Rate Swap: An exchange of cash flows based upon different interest rate indices denominated in the same currency on a pre-set notional amount with a predetermined schedule of payments and calculations. Usually, one counterparty will receive fixed flows in exchange for making floating payments.

Intrinsic Value: The economic value of a financial contract, as distinct from the contract's time value. One way to think of the intrinsic value of the financial contract is to calculate its value if it were a forward contract with the same delivery date. If the contract is an option, its intrinsic value cannot be less than zero.

Knock-in Option: An option the existence of which is conditional upon a pre-set trigger price trading before the option's designated maturity. If the trigger is not touched before maturity, then the option is deemed not to exist.

Knock-out Option: An option the existence of which is conditional upon a pre-set trigger price trading before the option's designated maturity. The option is deemed to exist unless the trigger price is touched before maturity.

Legal Risk: The general potential for loss due to the legal and regulatory interpretation of contracts relating to financial market transactions.

LIBOR (London Inter-bank Offer Rate): The rate of interest paid on offshore funds in the Eurodollar markets.

Liquidity Risk: The risk that a financial market entity will not be able to find a price for one or more of its financial contracts in the secondary market. Consider the case of a counterparty who buys a complex option on European interest rates. He is exposed to liquidity risk because of the possibility that he cannot find anyone to make him a price in the secondary market and because of the possibility that the price he obtains is very much against him and the theoretical price for the product.

Look-back Options: An option which gives the owner the right to buy (sell) at the lowest (highest) price that traded in the underlying from the inception of the contract to its maturity, i.e., the most favourable price that traded over the lifetime of the contract.

M

Margin: A credit-enhancement provision to master agreements and individual transactions in which one counterparty agrees to post a deposit of cash or other liquid financial instruments with the entity selling it a financial instrument that places some obligation on the entity posting the margin.

Mark-to-market Accounting: A method of accounting most suited for financial instruments in which contracts are revalued at regular intervals using prevailing market prices. This is known as taking a "snapshot" of the market.

Market Risk: The exposure to potential loss from fluctuations in market prices.

Market-maker: A participant in the financial markets who guarantees to make simultaneously a bid and an offer for a financial contract with a pre-set bid/offer spread up to a predetermined maximum contract amount..

N

Naked Option Writing: The act of selling options without having any offsetting exposure in the underlying cash instrument.

Netting: When there are cash flows in two directions between two counterparties, they can be consolidated into one net payment from one counterparty to the other thereby reducing the settlement risk involved.

O

Open Interest: Exchanges are required to post the number of outstanding long and short positions in their listed contracts. This constitutes the open interest in each contract.

Operational Risk: The potential for loss attributable to procedural errors or failures in internal control.

Option: The right but not the obligation to buy (sell) some underlying cash instrument at a predetermined rate on a predetermined expiration date in a pre-set notional amount.

Out-of-the-money Spot: An option with no intrinsic value with respect to the prevailing market spot rate. If the option were to mature immediately, the optionholder would let it expire. For a call price to have intrinsic value, the strike must be less than the spot price. For a put price to have intrinsic value, the strike must be greater than the spot price.

Out-of-the-money Forward: An option with no intrinsic value with respect to the prevailing market forward rate. If the option were to mature immediately, the option-holder would let it expire. For a call price to have intrinsic value, the strike must be less than the spot price. For a put price to have intrinsic value, the strike must be greater than the spot price.

Over-the-counter: Any transaction that takes place between two counterparties and does not involve an exchange is said to be an over-the-counter transaction.

P

Path-dependent Options: Any option whose value depends on the path taken by the underlying cash instrument.

Potential Exposure: An assessment of the future positive intrinsic value in all of the contracts outstanding with an individual counterparty who may choose (or may be unable) to make their obligated payments.

Premium: The cost associated with a derivative contract, referring to the combination of intrinsic value and time value. It usually applies to options contracts. However, it also applies to off-market forward contracts.

Put Option: A put option is a financial contract giving the owner the right but not the obligation to sell a pre-set amount of the underlying financial instrument at a pre-set price with a pre-set maturity date.

Put-call Parity Theorem: A long position in a put combined with a long position in the underlying forward instrument, both of which have the same delivery date has the same behavioural properties as a long position in a call for the same delivery date. This can be varied for short positions, etc.

Quanto Option: An option the payout for which is denominated in an index other than the underlying cash instrument.

Regulatory Risk: The potential for loss stemming from changes in the regulatory environment pertaining to derivatives and financial contracts, the utility of these instruments for different counterparties, etc.

Rho: The sensitivity of a financial contract's value to small changes in interest rates.

Risk Metrics (Value-at-risk): A parametric methodology for calculating Value-at-risk using data conditioned by JP Morgan's spin-off company Risk Metrics that is most useful for assessing portfolios with linear risks.

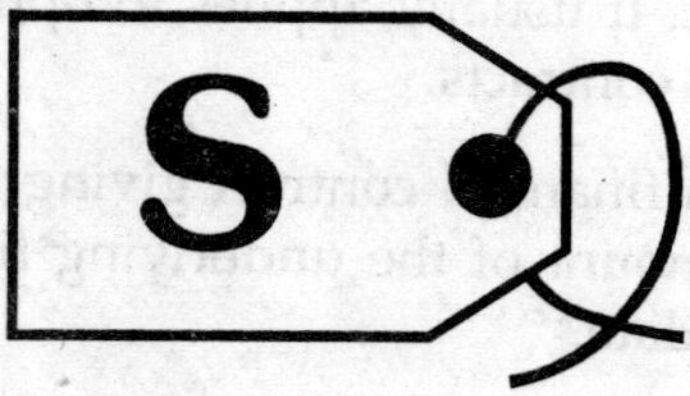

Settlement Risk: The risk of non-payment of an obligation by a counterparty to a transaction, exacerbated by mismatches in payment timings.

Speculation: Taking positions in financial instruments without having an underlying exposure that offsets the positions taken.

Spot: The price in the cash market for delivery using the standard market convention. In the foreign exchange market, spot is delivered for value two days from the transaction date or for the next day in the case of the Canadian dollar exchanged against the US dollar.

Spread: The difference in price or yield between two assets that differ by type of financial instrument, maturity, strike or some other factor. A credit spread is the difference in yield between a corporate bond and the corresponding government bond. A yield curve spread is the spread between two government bonds of differing maturity.

Standard Deviation: In finance, a statistical measure of dispersion of a time series around its mean; the expected value of the difference between the time series and its mean; the square root of the variance of the time series.

Stress Testing: The act of simulating different financial market conditions for their potential effects on a portfolio of financial instruments.

Strike Price: The price at which the holder of a derivative contract exercises his right if it is economic to do so at the appropriate point in time as delineated in the financial product's contract.

Structured Notes: Fixed income instruments with embedded derivative products.

Swap Spread: The difference between the swap yield curve and the government yield curve for a particular maturity, referring to the market prices for the fixed rate in a plain vanilla interest rate swap.

Swaptions: An option enters into an interest rate swap where a specified fixed rate is exchanged for floating.

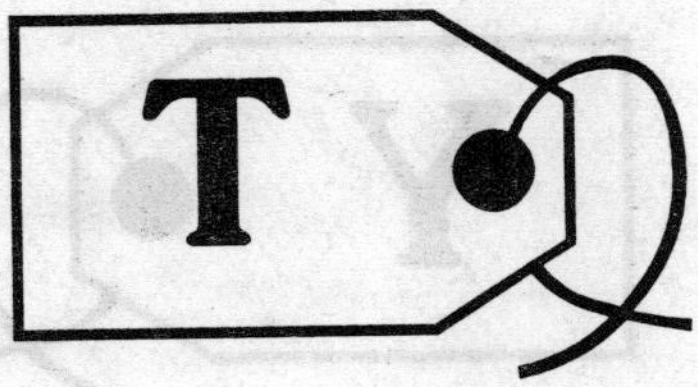

Theta: The sensitivity of a derivative product's value to changes in the date, all other factors staying the same.

Time Value: For a derivative contract with a non-linear value structure, time value is the difference between the intrinsic value and the premium.

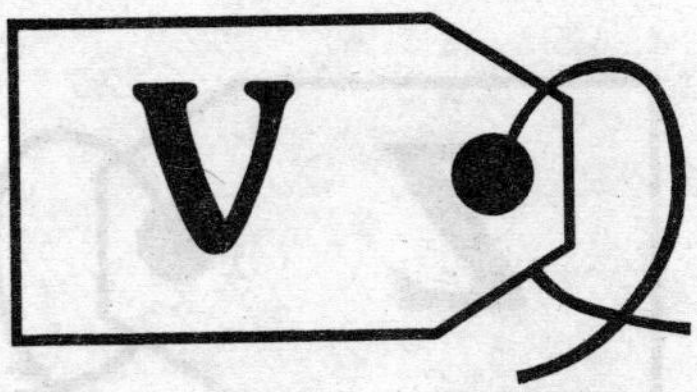

Value at Risk or VaR: The calculated value of the maximum expected loss for a given portfolio over a defined time horizon (typically one day) and for a pre-set statistical confidence interval, under normal market conditions.

Value of a Basis Point: The change in the value of a financial instrument attributable to a change in the relevant interest rate by one basis point (i.e., 1/100 of 1%).

Vega: The sensitivity of a derivative product's value to changes in implied volatility, all other factors staying the same.

Volatility: In finance, a statistical measure of dispersion of a time series around its mean; the expected value of the difference between the time series and its mean; the square root of the variance of the time series.

Y

Yield Curve: For a particular series of fixed income instruments such as government bonds, the graph of the yields to maturity of the series plotted by maturity.

Yield Curve Risk: The potential for loss due to shifts in the position or the shape of the yield curve.

Z

Zero Coupon Instruments: Fixed income instruments that do not pay a coupon but only pay principal at maturity; trade at a discount to 100% of principal before maturity with the difference being the interest accrued.

Zero Coupon Yield Curve: For zero coupon bonds, the graph of the yields to maturity of the series plotted by maturity.

End

4 Glossary: Capital Market Term

A

American Style Option: An option contract that may be exercised at any time between the date of purchase and the expiration date. Most exchange-traded options in the United States are American style.

Anticipatory Hedge: A trader expects to make a spot transaction at a future date and opens a futures position now to protect against a change in the spot price.

Arbitrage: Arbitrage is the practice of taking advantage of a price difference between two or more markets: striking a combination of matching deals that capitalize upon the imbalance, the profit being the difference between the market prices.

Arbitrage Band: Arbitrage band is the band around the no-arbitrage price, within which arbitrage transactions are not worthwhile.

Assignment: The receipt of an exercise notice by an option writer (seller) that obligates him to sell (in the case of a call) or purchase (in the case of a put) the underlying security at the specified strike price.

Ask Price: The price at which the market-maker is willing to sell. It also called the offer price.

At-the-money: In an option contract, at-the-money means if the strike price of the option is equal to the market price of the underlying security.

B

Back Months: The futures or options on futures months being traded that are furthest from expiration. Bear one who believes prices will move lower.

Backwardation: This occurs when the spot price exceeds the current price of a futures contract. The opposite of contango.

Basis: The difference between the cash price of a financial instrument and the price of a particular futures contract relating to that instrument. Also known as a crude basis or simple basis.

Basic Risk: The possibility that the value of the basis will change overtime.

Bear Market: A market in which prices are declining.

Bear Spread: A calendar spread designed to profit in a bear market.

Beta: The *beta* (â) of a *stock* or *portfolio* is a number describing the relation of its returns with that of the *financial market* as a whole. An asset with a beta of 0 means that its price is not at all correlated with the market. A positive beta means that the asset generally follows the market and a negative beta shows that the asset inversely follows the market. Generally, beta is measures systematic risk of the market.

Bid-ask Bounce: In the absence of new information, the transaction prices for a security will fluctuate between the bid and the ask price, depending on whether the trade was initiated by a buyer or a seller.

Bid-ask Spread: The difference between the ask price and bid price.

Bid Price: The price at which a market-maker is willing to buy.

Broker: A person who acts as an agent for others in buying and selling futures contracts in return for a commission.

Bull Market: A market in which prices are rising.

Bull Spread: A calendar spread designed to profit from a bull market.

Buy on Close: To buy at the end of a trading session at a price within the closing range.

Buy on Opning: To buy at the beginning of a trading session at a price within the opening range.

C

Calendar Spread: The simultaneous purchase and sale of futures contracts for different delivery months of the same financial instrument. Also called an intracommodity spread, a horizontal spread or a time spread.

Capped-style Option: A capped option is an option with an established profit cap. The cap price is equal to the option's strike price plus a cap interval for a call option or the strike price minus a cap interval for a put option. A capped option is automatically exercised when the underlying security closes at or above (for a call) or at or below (for a put) the option's cap price.

CAPM: Capital Assets Pricing Model. The equilibrium expected return on an asset depends on the riskless interest rate, the expected return on the market and the asset's beta (B) value.

Carrying Charges: The total cost of carrying an asset forwards in time, including storage, insurance and financing costs.

Cascade Theory: An arbitrage transaction where the trader holds a long position in the underlying asset and a short position in the corresponding futures contract.

Capital Market: Capital market is a source from which long-term capital is raised for the setting up the sustained growth of companies. The stock exchange is a part of the capital market, not only because it readily provides money for new or existing ventures, but also because it helps investors to trade in their shares and maintains the liquidity of investments.

Cash Market: In commodities markets this term is used to refer to the market in a particular grade and location of the underlying asset. For index futures there is only one underlying grade and location, and so the cash market is synonymous with the spot market.

Cash Settlement: Cash settlement is a settlement method used in certain futures and option contracts whereby, upon expiry or exercise, the seller of the financial instrument does not deliver the actual but transfers the associated cash position.

CFTC: Commodity Futures Trading Commission. An independent US federal agency which has regulated futures trading in the United States since 21st April, 1975.

Class of Options: Option contracts of the single type (call or put) and Style (American, European or Capped) that cover the same underlying security.

Clearing House: An organization connected with futures exchange through which all contracts are reconciled, settled, guaranteed and later either offset or fulfilled through delivery or cash settlement. Its function is to manage the margin and delivery systems, as well as to guarantee performance of exchange traded contracts.

Clearing Member: A member of the clearing house.

Closing Price: The last price of the trading period for a security.

Closing Purchase: A transaction in which the purchaser's intention is to reduce or eliminate a short position in a given series of options.

Closing Sale: A transaction in which the seller's intention is to reduce or eliminate a long position in a given series of options

Compulsory Close-out: A customer's open positions in futures contracts are squared-up by the member firm holding the account or the clearing house, usually after the customer fails to meet margin calls.

Condor Spread: A bull (bear) calendar spread in two different maturities is matched by a bear (bull) calendar spread in another two maturities. This requires there to be at least four outstanding maturities.

Contagion: Mistakes in setting prices in one market are transmitted to another.

Contango: This exists when the spot price is less than the current price of a futures contract. The opposite of backwardation.

Contract Month: The month in which futures contracts may be satisfied by making or accepting delivery.

Contract Multiplier: The monetary value that is multiplied by the index value to determine the market value of the futures contract.

Convergence: The movement to equality of the spot and futures prices as the delivery date approaches.

Corner: A few people gain control of all available supplies of the underlying asset.

Cost of Carry: The cost of holding a stock of the underlying, example, the costs of storing, insuring and financing the asset.

Counterparty: The other party either buyer or seller to a transaction.

Counterparty Risk: The risk the counterparty will not fulfil the terms of the contract. It also called default risk.

Cross Hedge: Hedging a risk is one asset by initiating a position in a different but related asset.

Crossing: A situation where the broker acts for both the buyer and seller. All cross trades must be transacted on the trading floor, or through the screen market but currently not allowed by SEBI in India.

D

Day Order: An order to trade futures contracts that automatically expires at the end of that day's trading session.

Day Trades: Trades that are opened and closed on the same day.

Default Risk: The risk that the counterparty will fail to meet their obligations under a contract.

Deferred Compensation: Deferred compensation is an arrangement in which a portion of an employee's income is paid out at a date after which that income is actually earned. Examples of deferred compensation include pensions, retirement plans, and stock options.

Deferred Contract: Futures contracts that settle in months beyond the closest current trading month. Also known as back contract.

Delivery: The transfer of ownership of an actual financial instrument, of a futures contract under the specific terms and procedures established by the exchange.

Delivery Day: The day on which the futures contract matures. It also known as expiry day.

Delivery Month: The calendar month on which the futures contract matures, resulting in delivery or cash settlement of the specified financial instrument. Also known as expiration month.

Delivery Price: The price fixed by the clearing house at which deliveries on futures contracts are invoiced. Also known as the expiry price or the settlement price.

Derivative: A *derivative* is a financial instrument and in simple it is an agreement between two people or parties — that has a value determined by the price of something called the underlying.

Double Auction Market: This occurs when the price is determined by competitive bidding between both buyer and sellers, as in futures markets.

Dual Listing: Futures contracts on the same underlying asset are traded on more than one exchange.

Dynamic Hedge: An investment strategy in which a long position in shares is hedged by selling futures and the futures position is adjusted frequently so that it replicates a purchased put option.

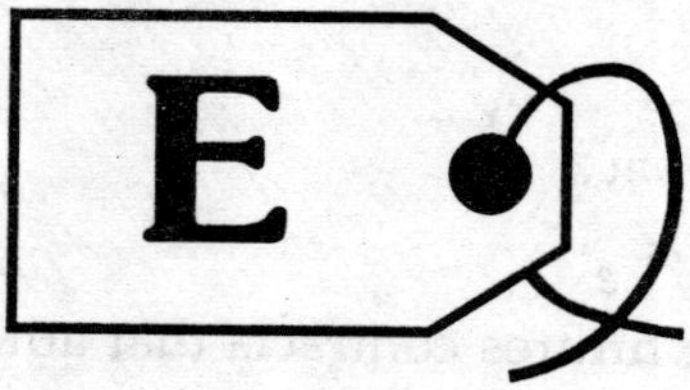

Efficient Frontier: The efficient frontier describes the relationship between the return that can be expected from a portfolio and the riskiness (volatility) of the portfolio.

EDSP: It stand for Exchange Delivery Settlement Price. The price at which the delivery or cash settlement takes place, expressed in index points and this terminology is common in the US.

Equity Options: Options on shares of an individual common stock called as equity options.

European Style Options: An option contract that may be exercised only during a specified period of time just prior to its expiration.

Equity Swap: A contract between two parties by which they swap the returns from an equity portfolio and an investment at a fixed or variable interest rate.

Exercise: To implement the right under which the holder of an option is entitled to buy (in the case of a call) or sell (in the case of a put) the underlying security.

Exercise Settlement Amount: The difference between the exercise price of the option and the exercise settlement value of the index on the day an exercise notice is tendered, multiplied by the index multiplier.

Expiration Cycle: An expiration cycle relates to the dates on which options on a particular underlying security expire. A given option will be assigned to one of three cycles, the January cycle, the February cycle or the March cycle.

Expiration Date: Date on which an option and the right to exercise it.

Expiration Time: The time of day by which all exercise notices must be received on the expiration date.

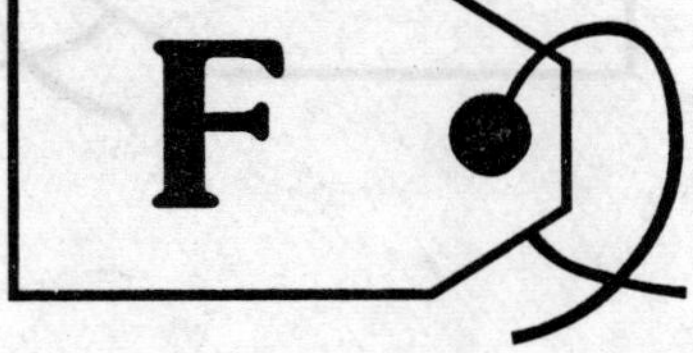

Far Contract: Far contract means the future that is furthest from its delivery month, i. e., has the longest maturity.

Fill or kill Order: An order to trade futures contracts which must be executed immediately called as killed order.

Financial Engineering: The process of designing new financial instruments, especially derivative securities.

Float Capitalization: The value of that portion of the firm's equity that is available for trading, and so excludes shares in the hands of controlling investors.

Floor Broker: An exchange member who is paid a fee for executing orders for clearing members or their customers. A floor broker executing orders must be licensed by the exchange where is working on.

Floor Trader: An exchange member who generally trades only for his/her own account or for an account controlled by him/her.

Forward Contract: An agreement between two parties to trade an asset at a specified future date and price. This is an OTC product.

Fundamental Analysis: The application of economic analysis to publicly available information to predict price movements.

Futures Contract: A legal, transferable standardized contract that represents an agreement to buy or sell a quantity of a standardized asset at a predetermined delivery date. This is an exchange-traded product.

Futures Option: An option written on a futures contract is called as futures option.

Hedge: In simple hedge means a trade designed to reduce risk. A spread between a spot asset and a futures position that reduces risk.

Hedge Portfolio: The portfolio of shares whose risk is being hedged away.

Hedge Ratio: The number of futures contracts bought or sold divided by the number of spot contracts whose risk is being hedged.

Hedging: The purchase or sale of futures contracts to offset possible changes in the value of assets or cost of liabilities currently held, or expected to be held at some future date.

Holder: The party who purchased an option is called as holder.

Holding Period: The time period over which an investment is held.

I

Implementation Risk: The risk that new information may arrive after an investors has decided to trade and before the order is submitted.

Implied Volatility: The variance of returns on an asset that is implied by equating the observed and theoretical prices of an option on that asset.

Index Fund: An institutional investment portfolio that aims to replicate the performance of a chosen market index.

Index Option: An option written on a stock index called as index option.

Index Participation: The trading of baskets of shares corresponding to those in some specified market index. The buyer of the index participation pays immediately in exchange for a promise by the seller to deliver the shares at one of a number of subsequent dates, chosen by the buyer. Also know as an ***Exchange Traded Fund (ETF).***

Initial Margin: The 'good faith' deposit of the cash or securities which a user of futures market must make with his or her broker when purchasing or selling futures contracts, as a guarantee of contract fulfilment.

Insider Trading: Dealing of trading on the basis of inside information called as insider trading.

Inter-market Spread: A spread involving futures contracts traded on different exchanges called as inter-market spread.

Intra-market Spread: A spread involving future contracts traded on the same exchange called as intra-market spread.

Invert-market Spread: A market in which the price of stock index futures is higher the closer is the contract to delivery.

In-the-money: In a call option contract, term in-the-money means, if the strike price is less than the market price of the underlying security. But in a put option, in-the-money if the strike price is greater than the market price of the underlying security.

K

Kerb Trading: Unofficial trading when the market has closed called as kerb trading.

L

LEAPS: Long-term Equity Anticipation Securities. These are relatively long-term stock or index options. LEAPS are available in two types, calls and puts and the expiration dates up to three years in the future.

Leverage Effect: When the price of a share rises and the value of the firm's outstanding debt is fixed, the ratio of debt to equity falls, i.e., its leverage (or gearing) falls. This makes return on the share less risky. A reverse argument applies for price falls.

Limit Down: It occurs when the futures price has moved down to the lower price limit.

Limit Move: The price has increased or decreased by the maximum amount permitted by the price limits.

Limit Order: An order to buy or sell at a specific price or a better price, to be executed when and if the market price reaches the specified price.

Limit-up: It occurs when the price has moved up to the upper price limit.

Local: A floor trader who executes trades on his or her own account in the open outcry system.

Long: A market position established by buying one or more futures contracts not yet close out through an offsetting sale; the opposite of shot.

Long Hedge: A hedge involving a long futures position and a short spot position.

Long Position: A position involving the purchase of an asset.

Long the Basic: The purchase of the underlying asset and sale of contracts in the corresponding futures contract.

Macro Hedging: A firm hedges the combined exposure of all its assets and liabilities.

Maintenance Margin: The minimum amount which a person is required to keep in their margin account.

Margin: A margin is *collateral* that the holder of a *financial instrument* has to deposit to cover some or all of the *credit risk* of his *counterparty* and this risk can arise if the holder has done borrowed cash from the counterparty to buy financial instruments or sold financial instruments *short,* or entered into a *derivative* contract.

Margin Call: A request for the payment of additional funds into a person's margin account.

Mark-to-market: The daily adjustment/settlement of margin accounts to reflect profits and losses.

Market Capitalization: It is calculated by multiplying the number of a company's shares issued by the share price.

Market Efficiency: The degree to which current prices reflect a set of information.

Market-maker: A dealer who makes firm bids and offers at which he or she will trade.

Market-on-close Order: An order to buy or sell at a price as close as possible to the closing price for that day.

Market-on-open: A market order to be executed during the opening.

Market order: An order to buy or sell for immediate execution at the best obtainable price.

Market Portfolio: A market value weighted portfolio consisting of every share traded on the exchange.

Market Risk: Market risk is the *risk* that the value of a portfolio, either an investment portfolio or a trading portfolio, will decrease due to the change in value of the market risk factors. The four standard market risk factors are stock prices, interest rates, foreign exchange rates, and commodity prices.

Marking to the Market: The daily revaluation of open positions to reflect profits and losses based on closing market prices at the end of the trading day.

Matching: The process by which buy and sell transactions are reconciled, before being passed to the clearing house.

Minimum Price Fluctuation: Smallest increment of price movement possible in trading a given contract, more commonly referred to as a "tick".

Micro Hedging: A firm hedges only specific transactions rather than all its assets and liabilities.

Momentum Trader: A trader who sells when the market falls and buys when the market rises. This behaviour tends to amplify price movements. Also known as a positive feedback trader.

N

Near Contract: The future that is nearest to its delivery month, i.e., has the shortest maturity.

Net Position: The difference between the long and short open positions in any one future held by an individual or group.

Non-synchronicity: The stock trades at least once every interval, but not necessarily at the close of each interval.

Normal Backwardation: It occurs when the expected price of a futures contract at delivery exceeds the current price of the future.

Normal Market: A market in which the price of a stock index futures contract is lower than the closer is the contract to delivery.

O

Odd Lot: A quantity of shares that does not correspond to that in which trading normally takes place.

Offer: The price at which an investor is willing to sell a futures or options contract.

Open Interest: The cumulative number of either long or short contracts which have been initiated on an exchange, and have not been offset.

Open Outcry: The method trading on many futures exchanges whereby bids and offers are audible to all other participants on the floor of the exchange in a competitive public action.

Opening Purchase: A transaction in which the purchaser's intention is to create or increase a long position in a given series of options.

Opening Sale: A transaction in which the seller's intention is to create or increase a short position in a given series of options.

Original Margin: The initial margin required to cover a new futures position called as original margin.

Out-of-the-money: In a call option the term out-of-the-money means if the strike price is greater than the market price of the underlying security. But in a put option, out-of-the-money if the strike price is less than the market price of the underlying security.

Out Trade: A trade for which there is not a matching record by the two parties. It may be because the prices, quantity, maturity, counterparty or sides fail to match.

Overnight Trade: A trade which is not liquidated on the same day on which it was established.

Overpriced: The actual futures price exceeds the no-arbitrage futures price.

Over-the-counter (OTC) Market: A market where dealing does not takes place at an organized exchange.

P

Perfect Hedge: A hedge where the change in the value of the future contracts is identical to the change in the value of the other asset or liability.

Physical Delivery: Settlement of a futures contract by the supply or receipt of the asset underlying the contract.

Pit: An octagonal or hexagonal area on the trading floor of an exchange, surrounded by a tier of steps upon which traders and brokers stand while executing futures trades in the open outcry system.

Portfolio Insurance: An investment strategy employing various combinations of shares, options, futures and debt that is designed to provide a minimum or floor value to the portfolio.

Position Limit: A restriction on the maximum number of contracts that can be held by a single trader at any one time.

Position Trading: A trading strategy in which a position is held for longer than one day.

Premium (options): An options price has two components. They are the intrinsic value and time value. Premium is often referred to as time value.

Premium (futures): The amount agreed upon between the purchaser and seller for the purchase or sale of a futures option. The purchasers pay the premium and sellers (writers) receive the premium.

Price Discover: The process by which a market usually the futures market reflects new information before another related market usually the spot market.

Price Limit: The maximum and minimum prices, as specified by the exchange, between which transactions may take place during a single trading session.

Price Range: The difference between the highest and lowest pricing during a given period.

Price Relative: The price at time t + 1 divided by the price at time t.

Put: An option contract that gives the holder the right to sell the underlying security at a specified price for a fixed period of time.

Quasi-futures Contract: This is the same as a futures contract, except that the payments of variation margin do not involve the full daily price change.

Queue: The sequence of potential arbitrageurs, in order of increasing transactions costs.

Random Walk: The theory that changes in the variable are at random; that is, they are independently and identically distributed overtime.

Realized bid-ask Price: The difference between the prices at which scalpers have bought and sold.

Reportable Position: The number of futures contracts above which one must report daily to the exchange or the CFTC the size of the position by delivery month and purpose of trading.

Reserve Cash and Carry: An arbitrage transaction where the trader holds a short position in the underlying asset and a long position in the corresponding futures contract.

Risk Premium: A risk premium is the minimum difference a person requires to be willing to take an uncertain *bet*, between the expected value of the bet and the certain value that he is indifferent to.

Round Lot: Quantity of shares that corresponds to that in which trading normally takes place.

Round Trip/Round Turn: The purchase or sale of a futures contract and the subsequent offsetting sale or purchase. Transactions costs are normally quoted on a 'round trip' basis.

S

Scalp: To trade for small gains, normally by establishing and liquidating a futures position quickly, often within minutes, but always within the same day.

Scanning Range: The largest price movement in the underlying security for which the clearing house requires cover.

SEBI (Securities and Exchange Board of India): The regulatory body for all participants in the securities and derivatives markets in India.

SEC (Securities and Exchange Commission): A federal agency charged with the regulation of all US equity and options markets.

Security Market Line: Line showing the relationship between a security's beta and its expected return.

Settlement Price: The price which the clearing house uses to determine the daily variation margin payments. It may differ from the price of the last transaction.

Sharpe's Measure: A measure of the risk adjusted performance of an investment. It is calculated as the excess return on the investment divided by the standard deviation of investment returns.

Short: A market position established by selling one or more futures contracts not yet closed out through an offsetting purchase in anticipation of falling prices; the opposite of long.

Short Hedge: A hedge involving a short futures position and a long spot position.

Short Position: An investor's position where the number of contracts sold exceeds the number of contracts bought. The person is a net seller.

Short the Basis: The purchase of a futures contract as a hedge against a commitment to sell the underlying asset.

SPAN: It stands for Standard Portfolio Analysis of Risk. This is a system for calculating initial margins on portfolios of options and futures.

Speculation: Trading on anticipated price changes, where the trader does not hold another position which will offset any such price movements.

Spot Market: The market in which the asset underlying the futures contract is traded, example, the stock market.

Spot Price: A derivation of 'on the spot' usually referring to the cash market price of a financial instrument available for immediate delivery.

Spread: The simultaneous purchase of one futures contract and sale of another, in the expectation that the price relationship between the two will change so that the subsequent offsetting sale and purchase will yield a net profit.

Stop Order: A market order to buy when the market price has touched a specified level above the current price, or a market order to sell when the market price has touched a specified level below the current price. It is also known as a stoploss order.

Strengthening of the Basis: It occurs when the futures price declines relative to the spot price.

Strike Price: The stated price per share for which the underlying security may be purchased in the case of a call, or sold in the case of a put, by the optionholder upon exercise of the option contract.

Strip Hedge: A trader takes the same position either long or short in a future for a series of delivery dares. It may be used to hedge a series of payments or receipts.

Synthetic futures: A combination of a long call option and a short put option, or debt and the underlying asset, that replicates the behaviour of a long futures contract.

Systematic Risk: The systematic risk also sometimes called as *market risk*, aggregate risk, or undiversifiable risk. The *risk* associated with aggregate *market* returns. It is measured for each firm by a 'beta' value.

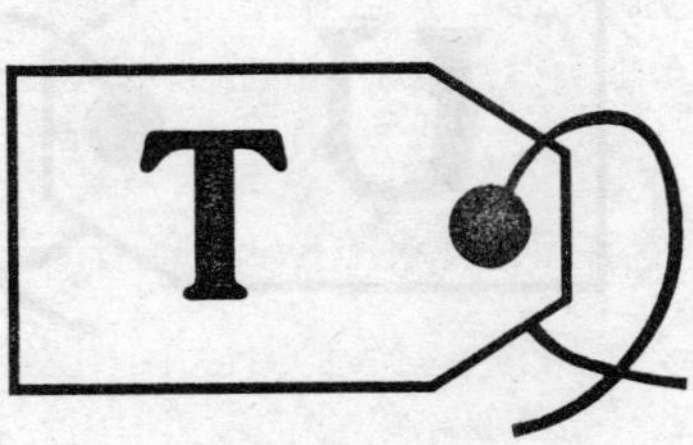

Tail Risk: The risk created by marking to the market called as tail risk.

Tailing Factor: The correction factor by which the hedge ratio is multiplied to allow for tail risk.

Tailing the Hedge: Correcting the size of hedge to allow for the risks of marking to the market.

Tax Timing Option: Capital gain or losses on shares are taxable when realized. The tax timing option refers to the fact that the owner can choose when to liquidate his or her position in the shares.

Technical Analysis: Technical analysis is a *security analysis* discipline for forecasting the future direction of prices through the study of past market data, primarily price and volume.

Term Structure of Futures Prices: The relationship between futures prices on the same underlying asset, but with a different time to maturity.

Thin Market: A market with few trades generally refers as thin market.

TIMS: It stand for Theoretical Inter-market Margining System. This another system for calculating performance bond requirements for options. It is developed by the Options Clearing Corporation (OCC).

Tick Size: Minimum permitted movement in the quotation. Measured in index points.

Time Value: Time value is whatever value the option has in addition to its intrinsic value and it often referred to as premium.

Tracking Error: Tracking error is a measure of how closely a portfolio follows the index to which it is benchmarked. The most common measure is the root-mean-square of the difference between the portfolio and index returns.

Trading Lag: The time delay between when an order is initiated and executed.

Trading Limit: The maximum number of contracts that a person can trade in a single day.s

Uncovered Call Writing: A short call option position in which the writer does not own an equivalent position in the underlying security represented by his option contracts.

Uncovered Put Writing: A short put option position in which the writer does not have a corresponding short position in the underlying security or has not deposited, in a cash account, cash or cash equivalents equal to the exercise value of the put.

Underlying Assets: An underlying asset is the asset on which the price of a *derivative* depends and most traded derivatives are settled for cash, not by actual delivery of the underlying.

Underpriced: The pricing of an Initial Public Offering (IPO) below its market value. When the offer price is lower than the price of the first trade, the stock is considered to be underpriced.

Unsystematic Risk: Unsystematic risk also sometimes called as *specific risk,* idiosyncratic risk, residual risk, or diversifiable risk. The risk which affect the company as specific or industry as specific risk in a *portfolio,* not the market as a whole. It can be removed by holding a well-diversified portfolio.

Uptick: An increase of one tick in the price of a security.

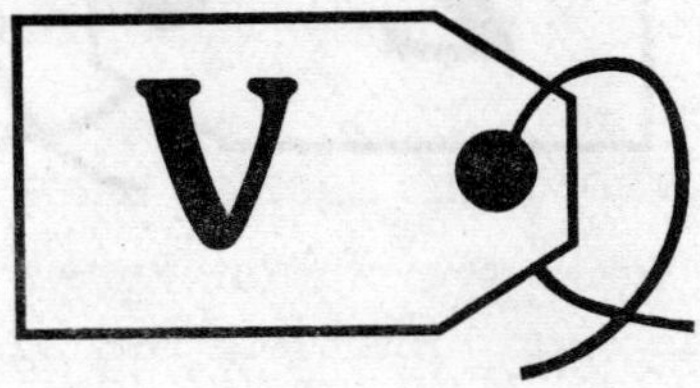

VaR: It stands for Value at Risk. A risk management methodology, which attempts to measure the maximum loss possible on a particular position, with a specified level of certainty or confidence.

Value Basis: The actual futures price less the no-arbitrage futures price called as value basis.

Value Trader: A trader who buys when assets look underpriced, and sells when assets look overpriced. Such a trader tends to buy when there is a large drop in prices, and sell when there is a large rise, and so tends to stabilize prices.

Variation Margin: The gain or losses on open contracts, which are calculated by reference to the settlement price at the end of each trading day and are credited or debited by the clearing house to the clearing member's margin accounts.

Volatility: A market is volatile when it's prices fluctuate a lot.

Volume: The number of transactions in a futures contract during a specified period of time.

W

Writer: The seller of an option contract called as writer.

Weather Derivative: Derivative where the pay-off depends on the weather.

Z

Zero-based Budget: ZBB is a budget in which the base is considered as zero and starting a budget at zero.

Zero-coupon Bond: It is called as a Deep Discount Bond (DDB). It is a bond which is issued at a discount and return it at a face value of the bond at maturity date. The difference between the discount price with the face value treated as the income or interested for the bondholder.

Zero-Sum Game: When the gains or losses of the long positions are exactly equal to the gains or losses of the short positions. It is true for the market as a whole for all futures products.

End

5 Glossary: Banking Terms

A

Accrued Interest: The accrued interest is the interest amount collected on purchase of bond or debenture since the preceding coupon imbursement, excluding the completion date. It included to the indenture price of a bond contract. There are two ways for computing accrued interest:

- On the basis of 360-day a year, employed for commercial and public shares
- On the basis of 365-day a year, employed for government shares.

Advance Payment: Compensation made to the indemnified person by the insurance firm prior to the completion date is called the advance payment. For instance, if the maturity dates of the claim is premeditated on July 1, 2004 and the insurance firm forfeits the petitioner before the settlement date, the payment is considered as an advance payment.

Allotment: Distribution of shares or bonds in support of new concerns is termed as Allotment. In other words securities allocated to associates of a countersigning consortium for the reselling to shareholders/investors.

Amalgamation: Amalgamation or consolidation is the procedure of merging or joining of two business entities into one new entity. The permutation can be an outcome of one business entity obtaining the other, uniting of two or more business entities, or either by suspension of obtainable firms and creation of a new firm to control the merged entities.

Amortization: It is also known as diminution, liquidation. In short, it is the distribution of an approximate amount during various durations, especially for mortgages and other type of investment which incorporates associated interest or other monetary charges. Amortization is generally used in determining the investment cost of securities.

Authorized Signer: An individual employed by the accountholder to sign and deliver cheques, demand drafts, receipts or any other form of payment in cash or kind is known as an authorized signer.

Automated Clearing House (ACH): An online money-transfer method established by the National Automated Clearing House Association is known as Automated Clearing House. This compensation method transacts in context of payroll, undeviating investment, tariff reimbursements, customer invoices, tax-fee and other payment facilities.

B

Bad Debt: If a particular bank or creditor fails to recover money from a borrower or a debtor, it is termed as bad debt. The bad debt is considered as an expense on the part of the bank.

Balance Transfer: Balance transfer is an option included in the application form of credit card. This facility is very useful for the person, who is holding more than one card. On availing this facility, the user can transfer the balance payable amount to the other card, if he/she is not able to make full payment that is due on a particular card. One needs to pay fee for the balance amount that has been transferred. The balance transfer facility is useful in reducing interest outgo.

Bank Statement: The savings accountholders receive passbook mostly. The passbook helps the accountholder to keep a track over his/her transactions. The account statement is nothing but like a passbook features all the transaction details on the person's account for a particular time period.

Banking Ombudsman: The banking ombudsman scheme is an efficient and cost-effective forum, which has been formed to resolve complaints registered by the customers in case of any services provided by the bank. The central bank of India namely Reserve Bank of India (RBI) has introduced this scheme under Section 35A of Banking Regulation Act, 1949. The scheme came into effect in the year 1995. RBI appoints the banking ombudsman, a senior official, to look into customer complaints in case of a particular banking service and resolve them.

Bounced Cheque Charges: A cheque can bounce on several accounts including inadequate cash in the account, signature mismatch and mismatch between the numerals and words. And if a cheque has bounced or has been dishonoured, the person who had drawn it needs to pay bounced cheque charges in that case. However, this is allowed only when the cheque has been returned due to insufficient fund in the account.

C

Cash Reserver Ratio: The part of the total deposits that is maintained in cash by the banks is referred to as CRR or Cash Reserve Ratio. The banks in India do not keep this part of their deposits with themselves. They need to submit this amount to RBI or currency chests. RBI has the right to decide on the minimum ratio of the deposits that need to be maintained by the banks.

Cash Back: The term 'cash back' is used in case of credit cards. Some of the banks that issue credit cards give back some money to the cardholder, if he/she uses the credit card to make payments at some particular retailers or merchandise stores. In the credit card statement, the user would get to know about the amount of cash back offered to him/her.

Co-branded Card: These credit cards are just like any other credit cards and can be availed from retailers or airlines apart from banks. A co-branded card user can gain travel points or avail attractive discounts related to the product. These cards are available in the sectors like telecom, travel, petrol pump, entertainment and retail. Nowadays, banks are offering co-branded debit cards also.

Clearing House: When a cheque is deposited in the bank, the receiving bank has to actualize the amount from the drawee bank before it is transferred to the concerned person's account. The drawee bank is presented with the cheque in the clearing house by the receiving bank. The clearing house is a main collection area for the banks to deal in financial securities including drafts, cheques and others.

Collateral: A loan seeker needs to provide collateral or the security to the lending institution. For example, in case of education loans, the seeker needs to furnish the lender with the collateral beyond a fixed amount. A collateral security can be referred to as the security that falls outside the limit of the loan.

Credit Appraisal: If a person applies for a particular loan, the lending institution runs a complete check on his/her credit profile to gather information on residence, age, occupation, service experience and the years of service as applicable to present job. Among these, the institution will also check if the person has taken any other loan. This entire process is referred to as credit appraisal.

Credit History: Credit History is a record of an individual's credit payment including borrowing and refunding of any kind of loans, credit cards, mortgages and any kind of debt that needs to be repaid. From credit history, a lender can know if the borrower had any late payment, bankruptcy or loan default issues. The Credit Information Bureau India Ltd., (Cibil) maintains these records and a lender can gain access to these details from Cibil as credit information report (CIR).

Credit Risk: When a lending institution grants loan to a customer, it assumes this risk. The banks ask for collaterals from the borrowers because of this risk factor. This risk factor is high in case of personal loans or any other form of unsecured loans. In addition, in case of secured loans such as home loans, the lender asks the borrower to share some portion of the risk, giving margin money. The interest rates are decided depending on credit risk. Interest rates are kept high, if loan involves high risk factor.

Debit Card/Credit Card: An ATM-cum-debit card allows an individual to purchase anything for the cash available in his/her account that is joined with the card, e.g., if a person has ₹ 5,000 in his/her bank account, he/she can use his card to the maximum limit of ₹ 5,000 only. On the contrary, credit card helps the user to do shopping till the assigned credit limit on that particular card.

Debt-equity Ratio: It helps in calculating the financial leverage of any bank or organization. To measure this, one needs to divide the total liabilities of the banks by stakeholders' equity. This in turn gives an idea of the ratio of equity and the debt used by the bank in financing the assets.

Default: If a person wants to continue his/her credit account, he/she either needs to give equated monthly instalments (EMIS) or pay the due amount on credit account each month within a fixed date. If the person fails to make payment before the specified date, it is considered as default. It can mar the credit record of that person.

Downpayment/Margin Money: When a bank asks the borrower to share a part of the credit risk and the payment that is received from him/her on this account, is referred to as down payment/margin money.

Direct Debit: Also referred to as Electronic Clearing Facility (ECS), direct debit option proves beneficial in case of servicing of various lines of credit. This is a facility whereby the person empowers his/her bank to take-off a particular amount from his/her account on a particular date every month.

Documentation Charges: The banks or lending institutions require certain documents from the person, who has applied for a loan, to look into his/her creditworthiness. The lending institution levies some charges for this purpose. These charges are known as documentation charges. The documentation charges are separate from registration charge, stamp duty and lawyers fee.

Dormant/Inoperative Account: If an individual has not made any transactions from his/her account for more than two years, a savings/current account is declared as inoperative or dormant.

E

Earnest Money: Good assurance amount of money allotted to seal an agreement is known as earnest money. For instance, in case of a contract to buy realty or an assurance fee to guarantee an advance payment of money by the lender, is referred as earnest money.

EFT (Electronic Fund Transfer): EFT or electronic funds transfer indicates to electronically supported systems employed to execute pecuniary operations by electronic means. EFT is used for a host of concepts such as credit/debit cardholder dealings, online payments by the cardholder, direct investment payroll compensations for some kind of dealing by a company to its members of staff, online bill payment, electronic Indian and international banking, etc.

Endorsement: Endorsement is a legal word that indicates to the signing of a credential which permits for the authorized transfer of a transferable amount from one person to another. In Insurance term, endorsement is referred to as rider, which acts as an inclusive prerequisite to an insurance strategy.

Expansionary Fiscal Policy: Guidelines implemented by the government to alleviate the financial system of the country, particularly, by regulating the levels and allotments of tariffs and government spending. During the phrase of slow-moving financial system, the government reduces tax impositions, giving extra privilege to taxpayers to elevate their levels of expenditure.

Expansionary Monetary Policy: The strategy implemented by the central bank of the country to control the cost and accessibility of funds and investments. They are implied to endorse economic objectives of a country either by increasing or decreasing interim interest rates, etc. When a nation undergoes deflation, the government orders to print more currency and circulate it in order to support inflation.

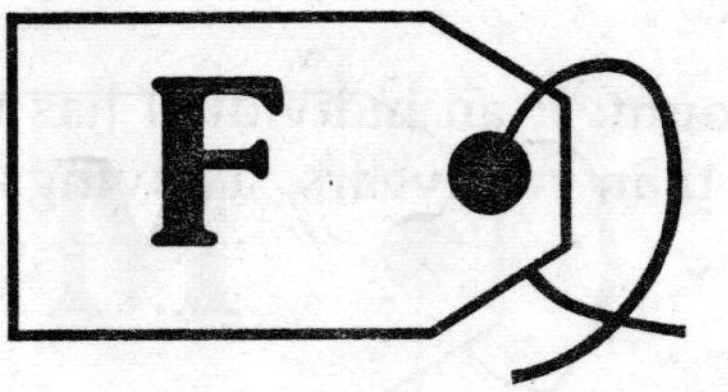

Free Credit Period: The free credit period is associated with credit. This period can be extended to 52 days. A person does not need to pay interest charges during this period, if he/she has made the full payment of his/her dues.

Fixed Rate: A fixed rate scheme means the interest rate has been specified for the full term of the loan. However, this scheme is not carried out in reality. The banks or lending institutions feature a clause that enables them to revise the interest rates after certain period of time.

Floating Rate: An interest rate that goes up and down periodically is referred to as the floating rate. Under the scheme of floating rate, the interest rate is influenced by the Floating Reference Rate (FRR) or Benchmark Prime Lending Rate (BPLR) of the bank. It implies that interest rate of the loan can change following the variations in FRR and BPLR.

L

Late Charge: A payment evaluated by the lender for a borrower and obtains it after a premeditated date is termed as late charge. Fine is implied for aberrant payments on a credit after a grace period of ten to fifteen days has passed. Late charge is computed as a proportion of the unpaid balance and is generally eliminated from the outstanding interest of the loan.

Leverage: The utilization of different fiscal tools or loaned capital to elevate the capability of potential profits from an investment is termed as leverage. In other words, leverage is an amount of debit utilized to fund a company's assets. A highly leveraged company comprises more obligations than equity. Leverage triggers investments on part of both investor and company.

Leveraged Buyout (LBO): The acquirement of a business entity by utilizing considerable sum of borrowed capital, through bonds or loans, to fulfil the expenses met during acquisition. Generally, the properties of the company being obtained are utilized as loan securities incorporating the properties of the obtained firm. The intention of leveraged buyouts is to permit firms to indulge in money-spinning acquisitions without entrusting a huge amount of money.

LIBOR: The LIBOR is an extensively used yardstick for interim interest rates. It is the rate at which privileged borrowers from all over the world are competent enough for borrowing money. LIBOR are also referred to the interest rates allotted for the less favoured world's borrowers.

Line of Credit: An understanding between a bank and a consumer ascertaining an utmost loan equilibrium that the financial institution can allow the borrower to retain is known as line of credit. The benefit of line of credit in case of ordinary loan is that the borrower is not entitled to forfeit on behalf of the portion of line of credit that he generally doesn't utilize.

Liquidation: When the operation of a company come to an end or when the company is considered as bankrupt, then its properties are sold, advance amount is paid to the creditors and surpluses are circulated to shareholders. In other words liquidation is referred to any kind of business deal that equalizes or terminates a short-term or long-term arrangement.

Liquidity Risk: The risks arising from the absence of profitability of an investment or deposit that can neither be purchased nor traded promptly to avert or reduce any kind of loss is termed as liquidity risk.

London Clearing House: London clearing house is an association related with an exchange to deal with the verification, payment and release of contracts along with satisfying the key responsibility of ascertaining that the dealings are done in a speedy and well-organized way.

M

MICR Code: MICR stands for Magnetic Ink Character Recognition. MICR code comprises nine digits given on the white strip in the lower part of the cheque on the right side of the cheque number. This is a unique code and no two bank branches can have the same set of this code in the nation. It facilitates the process of cheque clearance. The MICR code is different from the IFCS code that is mentioned on every cheque.

Minimum Quarterly Balance/Quarterly Average Balance: A savings accountholder needs to keep a minimum balance in his/her account on monthly or quarterly basis, as specified by the banks. In case of private banks, the person may have to maintain higher balance than that of any public sector bank. The public sector banks can ask a person to maintain a balance of ₹ 500 to ₹ 1,000. However, in private sector banks, the minimum limit for the quarterly balance begins from ₹ 5,000.

Moratorium Period: The moratorium period can be called a repayment holiday for loan. If an individual wants to secure disbursement of loan, but he doesn't have EMI or pre-EMI provision, he is provided with an option to dish out some amount, as stated in the bank policy. The moratorium period is contained in the maximum repayment period. An individual has to pay interest rates during this period.

N

Net Interest Margin: Net interest margin measures the success of the bank's decision taken in the area of investment as in case of debt situation. If the decision of the bank has not been fruitful, it denotes negative value. Negative value reflects that the interest expenses of the bank were higher than the returns coming from its investments.

No-frills Account: The apex Indian bank, i.e., Reserve Bank of India had issued an Annual Policy Statement 2005-2006 urging banks to take a look at their present practices to enable disadvantaged sections of the people to have an easy access to the banking services. These accounts witness limited number of transactions. Nowadays, almost every bank provides no-frills account to the customers. The central bank of India has made Know Your Customer (KYC) norms easy to facilitate the opening of a no-frills account.

NPA: The loans that can lead to a case of default are declared as Non-performing Assets (NPAs). If a person does not pay interest or principal amount for a period of 90 days, the loan is termed as a non-performing asset.

O

Obligation: The legal liabilities on a firm or individual to satisfy the conditions of an agreement. If the liability is not paid, the other party can resort to suitable measures as per the ones mentioned in the agreement.

Offer Price: Offer price is referred to the price which a purchaser is eager to acknowledge for a security. Besides the cost, the offer price usually specifies the sum of the security that the purchaser is willing to sell it for.

OFEX: OFEX or PLUS Markets Group PLC is a London-based stock exchange which emerged as a Recognized Investment Exchange in the year 2007. OFEX firms have greater tentative investments than Alternative Investment Market (AIM) firms.

Open-end Credit: A loan which was agreed previously and can be utilized frequently up to a definite limit is called an open-end credit. It also known as line of credit, it offers investors and firms an available amount of cash whenever required.

Open-end Fund: Open-end fund is a kind of mutual fund which includes no constraints on the number of shares the fund will allocate. In case of escalating demands, the fund will carry on allocating shares regardless of the number of investors. They can also be procured back and can be sold as per the desire of the investor.

Open-end Lease: A contract that compels the leaseholder, who make intermittent rent payments, to buy the rented property at the closing contents of the contract. It is also known as a "finance lease".

Out of the Money: Out of the money is a term which is used when the strike value of an option is greater than the market cost of the principal asset.

Outstanding Cheque: Cheque or demand drafts that have not been delivered to the forfeiting bank for compensation or the cheque which are still waiting to be collected are known as Outstanding Checks.

Over-the-counter (OTC): A security dealt in a different perspective other than the recognized stock exchange like NYSE, AMEX, etc. The term is associated with the stocks that are sold through a trader, the channel which is different from a federal exchange. It also indicates to the protection of the obligation and other fiscal tools such as derivatives, which are sold by merchants.

Overbought: It is referred to certain kind of condition in which the requirement of a specific asset excessively elevates the cost of the price of a principal asset to such an extent that does not assist the essentials.

Overdraft: Overdraft is regarded as an immediate expansion of credit from a loan providing organization. If the borrower has an overdraft bank account, his cheques would be covered by the banks in case if they bounce.

Overdue: Overdue refers to outstanding and more than outstanding amount which is postponed further ahead the premeditated time of arrival or imbursement.

Oversold: It is a situation in which the cost of the principal property declines rapidly to an extent of its original value. This situation is generally an outcome of panic selling of goods in the market.

Pin Number: A person needs to have pin number in order to gain an access to the ATM. This number is required, if the person is using credit card, ATM card or ATM-cum-debit card for the purpose of withdrawing money. Pin number is a set of digits that is sent by the bank to its customer separately after he/she receives the card. The pin number needs to be kept secret.

PLR/BPLR: PLR stands for Prime Lending Rate and BPLR for Benchmark Prime Lending Rate. PLR/BPLR is given to the main customers of the lending institution. Mostly, the rates of interest for all retail loans are connected with PLR/BPLR. However, in some cases, interest rates are dependent on the floating reference Rate (FRR).

Pre-payment Penalty: A person has to bear pre-payment penalty if he/she decides to close the loan amount ahead of time of its specified expiry date. This penalty is levied on the principal that a person owes to a lending institution. This penalty saves the lending institution from facing a loss of income generated through interest rates.

Processing Fee: A lending institution levies this fee in order to process the loan application of a person. This fee can be waived off during festive offers, if the lending institution so decides.

Repo Rate: If any bank faces fund shortage and seeks to borrow some amount from the central bank of India, i.e., RBI, it is charged the repo rate. If repo rate is reduced, the banks get to avail funds at low rates.

Reverse Repo Rate: When Reserve Bank of India takes fund from banks, it is charged the reverse repo rate. If reverse repo rate is raised, it becomes attractive for the banks to lend more money to RBI, as it accounts for higher interest rates.

RTGS, NEFT and IFSC Code: The National Electronic Fund Transfer (NEFT) system was started to facilitate the process of fund transfer from one bank to the other. RTGS or Real Time Gross Settlement, on the other hand, is a process which helps in money transfer from one bank to the other on gross basis and on a real time. This system makes money transfer fast and smooth. Settlement in real time implies that there is no waiting period for the fund transfer. Gross settlement, on the other hand, stands for settlement done on one-to-one basis. This is considered to be the full and final payment and cannot be revoked, as it is registered with RBI.

In order to ascertain the unique identity of the different branches of the banks, the Indian Financial System Code (IFSC) was devised. This code is a combination of letters and numbers. The first 4 characters of this code represent the banks code and next character includes the control character. Presently, 0 is used in the 5th position. The last 6 characters stand for the branch identity. In MICR code, one can refer to the nine numbers to locate a particular branch of the bank.

SARFESI Act: It stands for The Securitization and Reconstruction of Financial Assets and Enforcement of Security Interest (SARFESI) Act. It was introduced to offer an organized platform to the banking industry so that it can manage its increasing NPA stocks and also match the pace of foreign financial institutions. This act enables financial institutions as well as banks to acquire securities and deal in them. With the help of this act, the financial institutions as well as the banks can actualize the long-term assets and deal with the issues of liquidity. They can look for the mismatch in asset-liability and also get hold of their securities to better recovery. This act enables them to sell securities and bring down the number of Non-performing Assets (NPAs).

Savings Bank Account: A savings accountholder of a particular bank can carry out his/her banking transactions on daily basis. Mostly, these accounts are accessed for non-commercial purposes. Savings account helps is money withdrawal and cash or cheque deposits. A savings account user gets an easy access to ATM, mobile banking as well as internet banking.

Secured Loan: A secured loan is that against which the lender receives some sort of security from the borrower. Home loan is considered to be the simplest form of this type of loan. The interest rate on secured loans is less than the ones charged in case of unsecured loans.

Statutory Liquidity Ratio: The Statutory Liquidity Ratio (SLR) is a metric which enables the banks to know the minimum deposit percentage such as of cash, gold or any other form of security they need to maintain. It helps in controlling the credit growth in nation.

T

Time Decay: In simple, it is the process in which the cost of an option premium is worn as termination advances. It is also known as theta and time-value decay.

Time Deposit: Time deposit is a saving account or certificate deposit which is possessed for an allocated duration with the perceptive that the investor can extract it by providing written application only.

Time Value of Money: Also known as present discounted value, it refers to the concept that the capital available at a specific duration values much more than the similar cost in the future because of its prospective income ability.

Total Expense Ratio: A computation of the total value related to controlling and functioning of an investment organization such as mutual fund is total rxpense ratio. These values mainly incorporate organization charges and supplementary expenditures for instance transaction charges, official charges, assessor fees and other functional expenditures.

Total Return: The profit or loss on an investment that is accrued on two elements: earnings accrued from interest on dividends and capital expansion in the share value or bond value. Total return is generally expressed as a yearly proportion in context of the sum invested.

Treasury Bills: Treasury bills are an interim debt responsibility supported by the government with a maturity period of below a year. It indicates that the bond offers income to the holder rather than forfeiting of preset interest payments by the holder.

Treasury Bond: It is a profitable bond with a preset interest rate and a maturity period. The holder is entitled to make interest imbursements after every six months and the earnings accrued by the holders is only charged at the national level.

Treasury Note: Treasury notes are profitable investments with preset interest rate with a maturity period . They are widely preferred investments because they offer great derivative markets that trigger their liquidity. Interest fees on the notes are transacted after every six months till the investment matures.

Treasury Security: They are bonds which have a maturity level of more than ten years. Also known as 'the long bond', they uphold capital on a long-term basis and pays greater yields to the depositors.

Trendline: A line on the cost diagram of a security illustrating the general course of the development of a security in its business operations. Trendlines are used to investigate the cost of individual securities, like goods, mutual fund, etc.

Treynor Ratio: Treynor ratio was formed by Jack Treynor which computes surplus income accrued in comparison to the income which could have been accrued on safe investments for each unit of market instability.

Umbrella Fund: It is an investment phrase which is used to explain a combined investment policy presented in a form of one legal entity but incorporates many discrete sub-subsidizes which are sold as personal investment funds.

Underwriter: A legal entity which governs the unrestricted issuance and allocation of securities from a conglomerate or other issuing entity is known as an underwriter. Such kind of entity works in association with the issuing entity to verify the submission cost of the securities. It purchases securities from the issuing entity and trades them to depositors through the underwriter's allocation channel.

Uninsured Deposit: Uninsured deposits are not covered against losses. They generate greater interest rate due to absence of cover and the buyer undertakes all risks.

Unit of Trading: It refers to the usual quantity of shares, debentures, goods, equities that incorporates the lowest unit of buying and selling on an exchange.

Unit Trusts: A non-integrated mutual fund organization that permits accounts to possess assets and exceed gains via the accountholders, other than investing them again into the account.

Universal Stock Futures: An assortment of consistent futures agreements on the shares of respective firms is known as universal stock futures. The futures agreement is an accord between the purchaser and the vendor to purchase number of shares during any time in the future at a predecided cost.

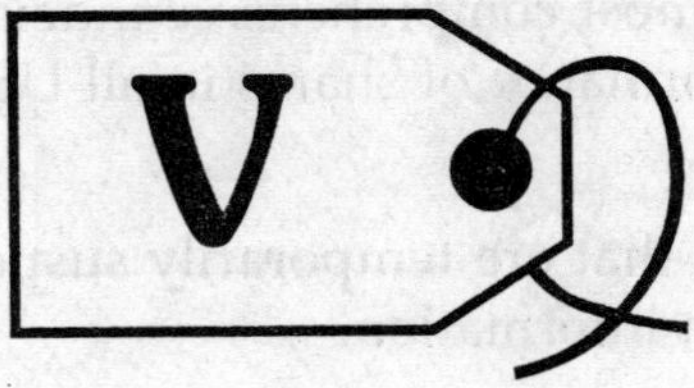

Venture Capital: Venture capital is a particular type of financing designed for new businesses (business start-ups). Start-ups are generally unable to access capital markets because they are private companies.

Vega: The vega of an option measures how sensitive the options price is to changes in the level of price volatility of the underlying instrument.

Vault Cash: Cash kept on hand in a depository institutions vault to meet day-to-day business needs, such as cashing chques for customers; can be counted as a portion of the institutions required reserves.

W

Warrant: A warrant is similar to a call option in that it gives the holder the right but not the obligation to subscribe for ordinary shares in a company. However, issued by the company itself and are therefore a liability to the shareholders.

Wilshire 5000: Probably the most comprehensive index of the entire US equity market: this index measures the performance of shares in all US-based companies with readily-available price data.

Withheld Deposits: Deposits that are temporarily suspended to be paid by the deposit insurer due to lack of enough information.

Withdrawal Penalty: A charge imposed upon an accountholder for the early removal of funds from a certificate account, usually an amount equal to interest earned during a pre-specified period.

X

XMI: Applies to derivative products. Quotron symbol for the Major Market Index (MMI).

Y

Yield Curve: A yield curve represents a snapshot in time of the yields offered by bonds of the same type and, in particular, of the same credit quality — but of different maturities.

Yield Spread: Yield - in whateverway it is measured — is the return offered on an investment. The yield spread is the difference between the yield on one security and that on another.

Yield to Maturity: Yield to Maturity (YTM) is the interest rate that, if inserted in the DCF price equation, makes the given price of the bond exactly fair. It takes into account not only the cash flows coming from the bond.

Z

Zoning: The creation of districts by local governments in which specific types of property uses are authorized (e.g., commercial, industrial, residential, high density, mixed use).

Zero-dividend Preference Shares: Zero-dividend preference shares are shares that pay no income, i.e., no dividend but have a fixed redemption value.

End

6 Accounting Abbreviation

A

Abbreviation	Stands For
A&AR	Accounting and Auditing Releases
A/C	Account Current
AAA	Accumulated Adjustments Account
AAA	American Accounting Association
AAA	Association of Accounting Administrators
AAA	Authentication, Authorization, and Accounting
AAA-CPA	American Association of Attorney — Certified Public Accountants
AACE	Audit Analysis Computer Environment
AACTS	Arthur Andersen Corporate Technology Solutions
AADA	Adjusted Attributable Deposit Amount
AADS	Account Authority Digital Signature
AAFA	American Association of Finance and Accounting
AAFI	Associated Accounting Firms International
AAG	Audit and Accounting Guides
AAGR	Annual Average Growth Rate
AAHCPA	American Association of Hispanic Certified Public Accountants
AAIA	Association of Airport Internal Auditors
AALC	Accountants and Actuaries Liaison Committee
AAMPS	Amtrak Accounting Materials and Purchasing System

AAMS	Automated Accounts Management Services
AAN	Accounting Audit Notation
AAOC	American Account Opening Centre
AAPR	Annualized Average Percentage Rate
AASD	Accountability and Accountancy Services Division
AATD	Alternative Amount of Tender Deposit
AATD	Australian Accounting Taxation Database
ABC	Accountability Basics and Control
ABC	Analyze Bill and Control
ABCD	Actuarial Board for Counselling and Discipline
ABOM	Accounting Business and Office Management
ABOM	Automated Bill Of Materials
ABR	Automated Budget Reallocation
ABREMA	Activity Based Risk Evaluation Model of Auditing
ABS	Accounting and Billing System
ABTEE	Annualized Before Tax Expense Equivalent
AC	Additional Charge
AC	All Current
ACA	Accreditation Council for Accountancy
ACA	Actual Cost Adjustment
ACAP	Accounting Career Awareness Programme
ACAT	Accreditation Council for Accountancy and Taxation
ACAT	Automated Customer Account Transfer
ACATS	Automated Customer Account Transfer Service
ACATS	Automated Customer Account Transfer System
ACB	Automated Clearing Bureau
ACC DET	Account Details

ACCC	American Consumer Credit Counselling
ACCPA	Atlantic Conference of Certified Public Accountants, Inc.
ACCS	Accounting Classification Code Structure
ACCS	Advanced Cash Control System
ACE	Accountability Creativeness and Efficiency
ACE	Accumulated Cash Equivalence
ACE	Adjusted Current Earnings
ACFO	Association of Canadian Financial Officers
ACH	Account Clearing House
ACH	Automated Check Handling
ACH	Automated Clearing House
ACMA	Alternative Compliance Market Account
ACMB	ABSA Corporate and Merchant Bank
ACMB	Accounting Control Management Behaviour
ACP	Activities Channels and Pools
ACP	Annual Compensation Payment
ACP	Anticipated Cash Provider
ACP	Average Conditional Probability
ACP	Average Contribution Percentage
ACPU	Average Cost Per Unit
ACR	Adjusted Community Rate
ACRA	Accounting and Corporate Regulatory Authority
ACRI	Accounting Careers Recruitment Initiative
ACRS	Accelerated Cost Recovery System
ASEC	Accounting Standards Executive Committee
ACT	Automated Credit Transfer
ACTS	Automated Card Tracking System

ACU	Automatic Client Update
ACV	Actual Cash Value
ACV	Annualized Contract Value
ACW	ATM Cash Withdrawal
ADD	Audit and Due Diligence
ADDACS	Automated Direct Debit Amendment And Cancellation Service
ADI	After Date of Invoice
ADIF	Accounting Data Interchange Format
ADJ	Adjust
ADL	Add Lot
ADM	Above Dealer MSRP (Manufacturers Suggested Retail Price)
ADM	Automatic Deposit Machine
ADP	Actual Deferral Percentage
ADP	Average Deferral Per cent
ADR	Accounting Department Revenue
ADR	American Deposit Receipts
ADR	Asset Depreciation Range
ADR	Average Daily Rate
ADS	Alternative Depreciation System
AE	Actual Expense
AEC	Annual Equivalent Capital
AEC	Average Efficiency Cost
AECC	Accounting Education Change Commission
AEI	Average Earnings Index
AEPU	Average Expense Per Unit
AEPU	Average Expense Per User
AER	Annual Equivalent Return

AEV	Alternative Equivalent Value
AFA	Accounting Firms Associated, Inc.
AFC	Average Fixed Costs
AFDA	Allowance For Doubtful Accounts
AFDC	Aid to Families with Dependent Children
AFE	Authorization For Expenditure
AFE	Average Funds Employed
AFF	Advanced Fee Fraud
AFI	Awaiting Faxed Invoice
AFIP	Association of Finance and Insurance Professionals
AFM	Accountancy and Financial Management
AFN	Additional Funds Needed
AFR	Applicable Federal Rate
AFS	Advanced Farming System
AFSC	AFSCME Financial Standards Code
AFT	Accounting, Financing and Taxes
AFTR	Applicable Federal Tax Rate
AFTS	Automatic Funds Transfer Services
AGA	Association of Government Accountants
AGI	Accounting Group International
AGI	Adjusted Gross Income
AGM	Adjusted Gross Margin
AGN	Accountants Global Network
AGR	Adjusted Gross Revenue
AICPA	American Institute of Certified Public Accountants
AIMS	Account Information Management System
AIRA	Allocated Insurance Reserve Account

AISG	Accountants International Study Group
ALCO	Asset/Liability Management Committee
ALE	Account Level Equivalence
ALF	Annual Licensing Fee
ALICE	The American Legislative Issue Campaign Exchange
ALLL	Allowance for Loan and Lease Losses
ALR	Active Life Reserves
AM	Account Monitoring
AMA	American Management Association
AMAP	Advanced Management Accounting Programme
AMT	Alternative Minimum Tax
AMTI	Alternative Minimum Taxable Income
AN	Account Number
ANCM	Assets, Non-current, Monthly
ANCQ	Assets, Non-current, Quarterly
ANP	Annualized New Premium
AOB	Angels Of Blind
AOI	All Other Income
AOP	Annual Operational Plan
AOT	Adjustment Of Terms
AP	Accounts Payable
AP	As Purchased
APA	American Payroll Association
APB	Accounting Principles Board
APBI	Accounting Principles Board Interpretations
APBO	Accounting Principles Board Opinions
APBS	Accounting Principles Board Statements

APC	Actual Payment Coefficient
APC	Annual Percentage Change
APD	Actual Profit Difference
APE	Annual Premium Equivalent
API	Accountable Property Inventory
API	Accountants for the Public Interest
APM	Accounts Payable Maintenance
APO	Automatic Payment Order
APR	Annual Performance Report
APR	Annualized Percentage Rate
APR	Automatic Payment Receipt
APTF	Accounting Policy Task Force
APY	Annual Percentage Yield
AR	Account Review
AR	Annual Return
AR	Auto Regressive
ARA	Accounting Research Association
ARA	Agency Reimbursement Amount
ARAF	Associated Regional Accounting Firm
ARB	Accounting Research Bulletins
ARC	Accounting Regulatory Committee
ARIA	Accounting Researchers International Association
ARM 3/1	Adjustable Rate Mortgage, 3 years overall, adjustable every 1 year
ARN	Account Reference Number
ARO	After Receipt of Order
ARO	Asset Retirement Obligation
ARO	Attribute Resolution Order

ARP	Automatic Remittance Processing
ARPU	Average Retail Per User
ARPU	Average Revenue Per Unit
ARSC	Accounting and Review Services Committee
ARTC	Accounts Receivable Truncated Cheques
ARV	Approximate Retail Value
ARV	Average Retail Value
ASAE	American Society of Association Executives
ASB	Auditing Standards Board
ASCII	American Standard Code for Information Interchange
ASET	Anonymous and Secure Electronic Transaction
ASLGU	Audits of State and Local Governmental Units
ASM	Account Services Management
ASQ	Allowable Sale Quantity
ASQ	Annual Saleable Quantity
ASR	Accounting Series Releases
ASWA	American Society of Women Accountants
AT	After Tax
AT	Automatic Transfer
ATB	Accounting Terminology Bulletins
ATC	Accountancy Training Centre
ATC	Average Total Costs
ATF	After The Flat
ATL	Above The Line
ATO	Asset Turnover
ATRA	American Tort Reform Association
AUD-SOP	Auditing Standards Division Statements of Position

AUDSEC	Auditing Standards Executive Committee
IAUG	Industry Audit Guides
AUI	Auditing Interpretations
AURA	Accounting Unit Reporting Application
AV	Accepted Value
AV	Actual Value
AVC	Account Validation Cheques
AVC	Added Voluntary Contribution
AVC	Average Variable Costs
AW	Assessed With
AWCA	African Women Chartered Accountants
AWCF	Army Working Capital Fund
AWP	Average Wholesale Price
AWS	Annual Wage Supplement
AWSCPA	American Woman's Society of Certified Public Accountants
AWW	Average Weekly Wages

B

BCE	Balance
B/O	On Behalf Of
BA	Balance Accounting
BA	Banker's Acceptance
BA	Business Associate
BAC	Budgeted At Completion
BACS	Bank Automated Clearing System
BARS	Budgeting Accounting and Reporting Systems
BAS	Business Activity Statement
BAVL	Budget Availability
BBA	Basic Banking Account
BBA	Budget Balance Available
BBAISR	British Bankers Association Interest Settlement Rate
BBP	Budgeting and Business Planning
BBR	Best Bank Rate
BC	Before Credit
BC	Budget Constraint
BC	Buying Criteria
BCBS	Basel Committee on Banking Supervision
BCD	Balancing Charge Debit
BCD	Book Closer Date
BCIJ	Best Cost Individual Join

BCL	Bank Credit Letter
BD	Bank Draft
BE	Bill of Exchange
BE	Budget Entity
BEAM	Bonds, Equity, And Money
BEP	Break Even Point
BES	Bill Enquiry System
BF	Bankruptcy Failure
BFI	Business Fixed Investment
BFP	Basic Formula Price
BG	Bank Guarantee
BIC	Bank Identification Code
BIC	Bank Identifier Code
BIC	Beginning Invested Capital
BIMBO	Buy In Management Buy Out
BIN	Bank Identification Number
BIPS	Bank Internet Payment System
BIR	Banking Intermediation Rate
BL	Bottom Line
BLR	Base Lending Rate
BOA	Bank of America
BOE	Barrels of Oil Equivalent
BOM	Bill of Materials
BOQ	Bill of Quantities
BOS	Bill of Sale
BP	Billing Provider

BP	Budget Power
BPI	Building Price Index
BPR	Business Process Re-engineering
BRASS	Bankruptcy Remote Access Server System
BRB	Beam Related Background
BRI	Bank Rakyat Indonesia
BS	Balance Sheet
BS	Bigger Surpluses
BSI	Billing System Investigation
BTA	Business Travel Allowance
BTP	Billing Transformation Programme
BU	Base Unit
BV	Book Value

C

C	Costs
C&F	Cost and Freight
CA(SA)	Chartered Accountant (South Africa)
CAAT	Computer Assisted Auditing Technique
CAD	Current Account Deficit
CAF	Common Assessment Framework
CAF	Credit Application Format
CAFR	Comprehensive Annual Financial Report
CAG	Cost Ascertainment Group
CAGR	Compound Annual Growth Rate
CAGR	Cumulative Aggregate Gross Revenue
CAIS	Credit Account Information Sharing
CAM	Credit Accumulation Mechanism
CAP	Competency Assessment Programme
CAP	Customer Approved Payment
CAPEX	Capital Expansion
CAPEX	Capital Expenditure
CAPM	Capital Assets Pricing Model
CAPPS	Computerized Accounts Payable And Purchasing System
CAPS	Corporate Accounts Payable System
CAPS	Credit Assessment And Programme Specifications
CAR	Capital Acquisition Request

CAR	Capital Adequacy Ratio
CAR	Compound Annual Return
CAR	Compounded Annual Rate
CAR	Cumulative Abnormal Returns
CAR	Cumulative Average Return
CARD	Certificate for Amortizing Revolving Debt
CARR	Compound Annual Rate of Return
CART	Committee Appointed Review Team
CAS	Composite Accounting System
CAS	Comprehensive Annual Statement
CAS	Cost Accounting Standards
CASA	Canadian Alliance of Student Associations
CASA	Citizens Assessment of Structural Adjustment
CASA	Clinic Assessment Software Application
CASA	Current Accounts and Saving Accounts
CASB	Cost Accounting Standards Board
CASH	Community Accountancy Self Help
CAT	Constant Amortized Time
CAT	Cost, Access, and Terms
CATS	Customer Account Tracking System
CB	Charge Back
CB	Cumulative Bulletin
CBA	Centrally Billed Accounts
CIBC	Canadian Imperial Bank of Commerce (Business Interest Account)
CBO	Congressional Budget Office
CC	Card Cash

CC	Cash Commodity
CC	Cost Centre
CC	Credit Card
CCA	Capital Cost Allowance
CCA	Capital Cost Annuity
CCA	Commercial Capital Access
CCA	Credit Card Action
CCAC	Cash Cheque And Charge
CCC	Credit Card Cheque
CCH	Commerce Clearing House
CCM	Check Control Module
CCP	Current COE Price
CCRA	Canada Customs and Revenue Agency
CCS	Cost of Common Stock
CCS	Credit Card Status
CD	Cash Disbursement
CD	Certificate of Deposit
CDC	Clearly Deceptive Calculations
CDCU	Corporate Debt Control Unit
CDFI	Community Development Financial Institution
CDIP	Certificate of Deposit Inflation Protected
CDM	Capital Derivatives Management
CDO	Collateral Debt Obligation
CDO	Collateralized Debt Obligations
CDO	Credit Default Option
CDS	Credit Default Swap
CDSC	Contingent Deferred Sales Charge

CE	Continuing Education
CEO	Costs Evened Out
CF	Cash Flow
CFA	Chartered Financial Analyst
CFA	Commercial Financing Advance
CFAB	Certificate in Finance, Accounting and Business
CFC	Controlled Foreign Corporation
CFCP	Cash Fund Control Plan
CFCR	Capital From Current Revenue
CFCT	Cash Flow Cycle Time
CFC	Central Finance And Contracting
CFM	Certified Financial Manager
CFO	Comprehensive Financial Optimizer
CFP	Certified Financial Planner
CFROI	Cash-Flow-Return On Investment
CFS	Cash Flow Surge
CFS	Comprehensive Financial Strategies
CFS	Corporate Financial System
CGAAI	Co-ordinating Group on Auditing and Accounting Issues
CGL	Commercial General Liability
CGL	Commonwealth Government Loan
CGR	Compound Growth Rate
CGS	Credit Gain Services
CHAPS	Clearing House Automated Payment System
CHFC	Chartered Financial Consultant
CI	Compound Interest
CIA	Cash In Advance

CIC	Chartered Investment Counsellor
CICA	Canadian Institute of Chartered Accountants
CIF	Common Interchange Format
CIF	Cost Insurance And Freight
CIMC	Certified Investment Management Consultant
CIMS	Certified Investment Management Specialist
CIP	Carriage and Insurance Paid
CIP	Central Investment Programme
CIT	Cash In Transit
CITC	Corporate Income Tax Credit
CLADR	Class Life Asset Depreciation Range
CLEC	Current Liabilities Exceed Cash
CM	Compounding Method
CM	Contribution Margin
CMA	Credit Monitoring Arrangement
CMBS	Commercial Money Bank System
CMFC	Chartered Mutual Fund Counsellor
CMK	Consumer Market Knowledge
CMS	Cost Management System
CMS	Credit Management System
CNC	Contract Negotiation Committee
CO	Charge Off
COB	Cost Of Borrowing
COC	Cash On Confirmation
COC	Cost Of Capital
COD	Cash On Delivery
CODA	Cash Or Deferred Arrangement

CODA	Cash Or Deferred Arrangement
COE	Cost Of Equity
COG	Cost Of Goods
COGS	Cost Of Goods Sold
COH	Cash On Hand
COI	Cost Of Insurance
COL	Cost Of Living
COLA	Cost Of Living Adjustment
COMET	Client Online Mortgage Enquiry Tool
COMPASS	Comprehensive Online Management Personnel And Accounting System For Sacramento
COP	Cash On Pick-up
COP	Cost Of Production
COPO	Central Order Processing Offices
COPS	Computerized Online Payment Service
COPS	Cost Of Produced Sales
COSI	Cost Of Savings Index
COSO	Commission Of Sponsoring Organizations
COSOTC	Committee Of Sponsoring Organizations of the Treadway Commission
COT	Carry Over Transactions
COW	Check Out Wizard
CP	Credit Points
CPA	Cheapest Price Available
CPA	Cost Per Action
CPA/PFS	Certified Public Accountant/Personal Financial Specialist
CPA/SEA	Certified Public Accountants/Society Executives Association

CPC	Customer Profit Contribution
CPE	Continuing Professional Education
CPF	Central Provident Fund
CPI	Cannot Pinpoint Inflation
CPI	Cardholder Payment Interface
CPI	Consumer Price Index
CPK	Certified Purchasing Knowledge
CPM	Critical Path Method
CPO	Confirmation of Purchase Order
CPP	Certified Professional Purchaser
CPR	Cash Position Recovery
CPR	Constant Prepayment Rate
CPRP	Cost Per Rating Point
CPS	Cash Payment System
CPS	Cost Per Sale
CPT	Central Payment Tool
CPT	Cost Payment Technique
CPTI	Core Pre-Tax Income
CR	Cash Receipts
CR	Cost Reduced
CRA	Cash Recovery Analysis
CRAC	Cost Recovery Adjustment Clause
CRO	Container Release Order
CROS	Cash Return On Sales
CRP	Cost Recovery Price
CRR	Cash Reserve Ratio
CRS	Cash Recycling System

CRS	Congressional Research Service
CRST	Coin Roll Storage Till
CSI	Capital Structure Irrelevance
CT	Converted Transaction
CTA	Corporation Tax Assessing
CTC	Cost To Company
CTC	Current Total Compensation
CTD	Cash Taken Deficiency
CTP	Corporate Trade Payment
CTR	Cash Transfer Report
CTS	Cash To Spend
CTX	Corporate Trade Exchange
CV	Complete Valuation
CVA	Cash Value Added
CVA	Combined Value Auction
CVP	Cost Volume Profit
CVV	Credit Verification Value
CVV	Credit card Validation Value
CWO	Cash With Order
CWO	Cheque With Order

D

DA	Duration of Asset
DB	Declining Balance
DB	Direct Bill
DBA	Date Book Archive
DBDP	Digits Before the Decimal Point
DCAA	Defence Contract Audit Agency
DCAP	Discount, Charges, Allowances, and Promotions
DCAS	Database Commitment Accounting System
DCCF	Discounted Cumulative Cash Flow
DCF	Discretionary Cash Flow
DCFPS	Discretionary Cash Flow Per Share
DCM	Debt and Cash Management
DCOH	Days Cash On Hand
DCOT	Domestic Corporation Occupation Tax
DD	Demand Deposit
DD	Demand Draft
DDA	Demand Deposit Account
DDB	Double Declining Balance
DDD	Desired Delivery Date
DEB	Debenture
DEL	Deletion
DEL	Departmental Expenditure Limit

DF	Discount Factor
DFAS	Defence Finance and Accounting Service
DFC	Down From Cost
DID	Data Item Description
DIF	Data Interchange Format
DIO	Days Inventory On-hand
DIR	Deposit Item Returned
DIRT	Deposit Interest Retention Tax
DISC	Domestic International Sales Corporation
DITL	Deferred Income Tax Liability
DIV	Dividend
DM	Debit Margin
DMD	Domestic Manufacturing Deduction
DMP	Debt Management Plan
DN	Debit Note
DNI	Distributable Net Income
DNS	Database of Names and Salaries
DOD	Debt Outstanding Disbursed
DP	Down Payment
DPO	Days Payable Outstanding
DPO	Departmental Purchase Order
DPP	Direct Product Profit
DPR	Data Production Request
DR	Daily Rate
DR	Discrepancy Report
DRC	Departmental Running Costs
DRC	Direct Responsible Charge

DRP	Debt Reduction Programme
DSC	Debt Service Coverage
DSC	Deferred Sales Charge
DSC	Designated Secured Creditor
DSM	Direct Sales Margin
DSO	Day Sales Outstanding
DSO	Days Sales Outstanding
DSRI	Days in Sales Receivables Index
DT	Debt Total
DTI	Debt To Income
DTR	Daily Trade Returns
DTS	Dock To Stock
DTTN	Digital Trade Transport Network
DUS	Dollar Unit Sampling

E

EA	Expenditure Authorization
EAA	Equivalent Annual Annuity
EAC	Estimate At Completion
EAF	Employment Administration Fund
EAP	Estimated Adjusted Price
EAR	Equivalent Annual Rate

EASA	Easy Access Savings Account
EAU	Estimated Annual Usage
EAY	Effective Annual Yield
EBG	Emirates Bank Group
EBIDT	Earnings Before Interest, Depreciation, and Taxes
EBIT	Earnings Before Interest and Taxes
EBITA	Earnings Before Interest Taxes And Amortization
EBITDA	Earnings Before Interest, Taxes, Depreciation, and Amortization
EBITDAR	Earnings Before Interest, Taxes ,Depreciation, Amortization and Rent
EBPP	Electronic Bill Presentment and Payment
EBT	Earnings Before Taxes
EBV	Economic Book Value
EC	Electronic Cash
EC	Electronic Commerce
ECB	External Commercial Borrowing
ECCO	Evaluation Of Capital Creation Options
ECI	Employment Cost Index
ECR	Efficient Cost Reduction
ECR	Electronic Cheque Recovery
ECR	Energy Cost Recovery
ECS	Electronic Clearing Service
ECTS	European Credit Transfer System
EDC	Embedded Direct Costs
EDD	Electronic Direct Deposit
EDF	Expected Default Frequency
EDMAX	Educational Management Exchange
EDP	Electronic Data Processing

EDPAA	EDP Auditors' Association
EDPAF	EDP Auditors' Foundation
EFS	Effective Financing Statement
EFS	Electronic Fund Systems
EFTPOS	Electronic Funds Transfer Point Of Sale
EFTPS	Electronic Federal Tax Payment System
EFTS	Electronic Funds Transfer System
EIC	Earned Income Credit
EIR	Effective Interest Rate
EIRF	Electronic Interchange Reimbursement Fee
EIRR	Economic Internal Rate of Return
EITC	Earned Income Tax Credit
ELMI	Electronic Money Institution
ELSS	Equity Linked Saving Schemes
EM	Electronic Money
EMI	Equal Monthly Instalment
EMI	Equated Monthly Instalment
EML	Estimated Maximum Loss
EMO	Electronic Money Order
EMO	Excess Manufacturing Overrun
EMV	Electronic Money Value
EMV	Expected Monetary Value
ENOD	Electronic Notice Of Deposit
EOF	Enterprise Object Framework
EOM	End Of Month
EP	Economic Profit
EP	Expensive Price

EPA	Equity Principal Additions
EPC	Earnings Per Click
EPC	External Processing Cost
EPO	Electronic Payment Order
EPO	Express Payment Option
EPS	Electronic Payment System
EQP	End Quantity Pricing
ER	Explicit Rate
ERA	Electronic Remittance Advice
ERA	Expected Rate of Advance
ERC	Equity Reciprocity and Competition
ERG	Emergency Response Group
ERISA	Employee Retirement Income Security Act of 1974
ERMA	Electronic Recording Machine Accounting
ERR	External Rate of Return
ERTA	Economic Recovery Tax Act of 1981
ESCA	Electronic Smart Card Account
ESOP	Employee Stock Option Plan
ET	Earning Threshold
ET	Employment Tax
ETA	Electronic Transfer Account
EV	Enterprise Value
EV	Exposure Value
EVA	Economic Value Added
EVA	Express Value Account
EVMS	Earned Value Management System
EY	Ernst & Young

F

F	Fireproof
F	Fiscal
F	Foreclosure
FAACS	Fixed Asset Accounting and Control System
FAB	Finance Advisory Board
FAB	Fulfilment Assurance and Billing
FACS	Financial Activity Control System
FACTS	Fast Automatic Cash Transfer System
FADM	Financial Accounting Database Management
FAE	Foundation for Accounting Education
FAF	Financial Accounting Foundation
FAO	For Account Of....
FARM	Financial Analysis For Retail Management
FAS	Financial Accounting Standards
FASAB	Federal Accounting Standards Advisory Board
FASAC	Financial Accounting Standards Advisory Committee
FASB	Financial Accounting Standards Board
FASBI	Financial Accounting Standards Board Interpretations
FASB	Statements of the Financial Accounting Standards Board
FASBT	Financial Accounting Standards Board Technical Bulletins
FBC	Foreign Bank Charges
FBO	Final Buy Out

FBO	For the Benefit Of....
FBS	Finance and Business Services
FBT	Fringe Benefit Tax
FBU	Finance Bank Utility
FC	Finance Charge
FC	Financial Capital
FCA	Fellow Chartered Accountant
FCE	Final Consumption Expenditure
FCF	Free Cash Flow
FCPA	Foreign Corrupt Practices Act
FDBD	Foreign Documentary Bills Discounted
FDC	Fees, Deposits, and Credits
FDD	Foreign Demand Draft
FDIC	Federal Deposit Insurance Corporation
FDR	Federal Deposit Reimbursement
FE	Fiscal Equalization
FEI	Financial Executives Institute
FEITFIS	FASB Emerging Issues Task Force Issue Summaries
FERF	Financial Executives Research Foundation
FFIEC	Federal Financial Institutions Examination Council
FFO	Funds From Operations
FGAA	Federal Government Accountant's Association
FICA	Federal Insurance Contributions Act
FID	Financial Information Data
FIDO	Financial Information Delivered Online
FIND	Financial Information Net Directory
FIRE	Finance Insurance And Real Estate

FIS	Financial Information Strategy
FIS	Financial Information System
FIS	Free In Store
FL	Financial Loss
FMA	Financial Management Assessment
FMCG	Financial Management for Consumer Goods
FMS	Fraud Management System
FMSS	Financial Management Software System
FMSS	Financial Management Systems Software
FN	Fiscal Note
FOB	Free On Board
FOC	Firm Order Commitment
FOFI	Future Oriented Financial Information
FOMC	Federal Open Money Committee
FOP	Form Of Payment
FP	Floating Point
FPA	Financial Performance Assessment
FPA	Full Page Ad
FR	Federal Register
FRB	Federal Reserve Bank
FRO	From Receipt of Order
FRR	Facility Risk Rating
FRR	Financial Reporting Releases
FRS	Financial Records System
FS	Fact Sheet
FS	Financial Statement
FSA	Federation of Schools of Accountancy

FSA	Flexible Spending Arrangement
FSAP	Financial Statement Analysis Package
FSAQ	Financial Statement Analysis Questionnaire
FSC	Foreign Sales Corporation
FSP	Flexible Spending Plan
FSR	Financial Status Report
FT	Fair Trade
FTC	Federal Trade Commission
FTD	Federal Tax Deposit
FTM	Financial Tax Management
FTR	Financial Transmission Right
FTT	Foreign Telegraphic Transfer
FUTA	Federal Unemployment Tax
FV	Future Value
FVAN	Future Value Annuity
FVF	Final Value Fee
FWP	Factory Wholesale Price

G

GAAFR	Governmental Accounting, Auditing, and Financial Reporting
GAAS	Generally Accepted Auditing Standards
GAF	Growing Annuity Factor
GAGAS	Generally Accepted Government Auditing Standards
GAM	Group Annuity Mortality
GAO	General Accounting Office
GAP	Guaranteed Asset Protection
GAR	General Accounts Receivable
GAS	Governmental Accounting Standards
GASB	Governmental Accounting Standards Board
GASB-COD	Governmental Accounting Standards Board Codification
GASBI	Governmental Accounting Standards Board Interpretations
SGASBS	Statements of the Governmental Accounting Standards Board
GASBTB	Governmental Accounting Standards Board Technical Bulletins
GB	Give Back
GC	Gizmo Cost
GCA	Global Cash Access
GDP	Good Debt Payments
GDS	General Depreciation System
GFIA	Governmental Financial Institutions and Agencies
GFOA	Government Finance Officers Association
GFS	General Finance Statistics

GJ	General Journal
GLI	General Ledger Interface
GLW	General Ledger Warehouse
GMAC	General Motors Acceptance Corporation
GMS	Gross Merchandise Sales
GMV	Guaranteed Minimum Value
GOP	Gift Of Propriety
GOP	Gross Operating Profit
GP	Guide Price
GPE	Gravitational Potential Energy
GR	Growth Rates
GRM	Gross Rent Multiplier
GTB	General Transaction Background
GTB	Global Transaction Banking
GTL	Group Term Life
GTT	General Agreement on Tariffs and Trades
GWS	Gross Wages and Salaries

H

HAM	Hold A Month
HD	High Dollar
HEP	Home Equity Prepayment
HFMA	Health care Financial Management Association
HLBV	Hypothetical Liquidation at Book Value
HNAG	Historical National Accounting Group
HP	Half Paid
HV	High Volume

I

I	Interest
IAA	Internal Accounting Association
IAD	Interest Adjustment Date
IAD	Interest Adjustment Date
IAFP	International Association for Financial Planning
IAG	International Auditing Guidelines

IAHA	International Association of Hospitality Accountants
IAI	Independent Accountants International
IAO	In the Amount Of
IAPC	International Auditing Practices Committee
IBAN	International Bank Account Number
IBDA	Independent Broker Dealer Association
IBM	International Business Machines
IBRD	International Bank for Reconstruction and Development
IBS	Internet Banking System
IC	Internal Control
ICA	International Congress of Accountants
ICAA	Institute of Chartered Accountants in Australia
ICAP	Institute of Chartered Accountants of Pakistan
ICFA	Institute of Chartered Financial Analysts
ICFP	Institute for Certified Financial Planners
ICM	Incentive Compensation Management
ICMA	Institute of Certified Management Accountants
ICR	Indirect Cost Recovery
ICR	International Credit Repair
ICS	Issuers Clearinghouse Service
ICSO	Internal Control Sarbanes-Oxley
ICST	Intra-company Stock Transfer
ID	Identification
IDB	Industrial Development Bond
IDC	Intangible Drilling Cost
IDC	Interest During Construction
IDCR	InDirect Cost Recovery

IDCRF	InDirect Cost Recovery Funds
IDRB	Industrial Development Revenue Bonds
IF	Intelligent Finance
IFPS	Interactive Financial Planning System
IFS	Industrial and Financial System
IFS	Institutional Financing Services
IG	Inspector General
IGAF	International Group of Accounting Firms
IIA	Institute of Internal Auditors
IIN	Institution Identification Number
ILOC	Irrevocable Letter Of Credit
IM	Instant Money
IMA	Investment Management Agreement
IMMA	Insured Money Market Account
INCFO	Institute of Newspaper Controllers and Finance Officers
ING	International Netherlands Group
IO	Interest Only
IOC	Insist On Cash
IOCR	Incremental Output Capital Ratio
IOCS	In-Office Cost System
IOLTA	Interest on Lawyers' Trust Accounts
IOU	Is Owed Unto....
IPC	Information Product Cash
IPO	Interest Paid On
IPR	Internal Purchase Requisition
IPS	Interactive Purchasing System
IPS	Interim Payment System

IPS	Internet Payment Solutions
IPS	Internet Payment System
IPS	Invoice and Progress Schedule
IPSAS	International Public Sector Accounting Standards
IPSP	Internet Payment Service Provider
IR	Income Ratio
IRA	Individual Retirement Account
IRB	Internal Ratings Based
IRB	Internal Revenue Bulletin
IRC	International Reply Coupon
IRC	Item Related Cheques
IRG	Interest Rate Guarantee
IRP	Intermediary Relending Programme
IRS	Increasing Returns to Scale
ISA	International Standard of Auditing
ISBA	Idaho State Board of Accountancy
ISBP	International Standard Banking Practice
ISO	Incentive Stock Option
ITA	Israeli Tax Authority
ITIN	Individual Taxpayer Identification Number
ITL	Interested Transaction List
IW	Instalment Warrant

J

JC	Just Cash
JE	Journal Entry
JEEP	Joint Ethics Enforcement Plan
JFS	Journal File System
JIB	Joint Interest Billing
JMI	Jointly Managed Inventory
JN	Journal Name
JPAS	JITC Project And Accounting System
JRN	Journal
JRTC	Job Retention Tax Credit
JV	Journal Voucher

K

KDT	Cost of Debt before Tax
KDX	Cost of Debt after Tax
KIBOR	Karachi Inter-Bank Offered Rate
KOA	Keep On Adding
KR	Key Rate
KVA	Knowledge Value Added

L

L	Liabilities
LAE	Loss Adjustment Expenses
LAR	Legal Amount Recognition
LASER	Loans And Savings Earn Rewards
LB	Logging and Bookkeeping
LBA	Loss Based Adjustment
LC	Letter of Credit
LC	Loan Commitment
LCM	Lower of Cost or Market
LCR	Loan to Cost Ratio
LE	Limited Expense
LE	Line Entry
LES	Linear Expenditure System
LESAC	Lab, Engineering, Sales, and Administration Costs
LEXIS	Legal Exchange Information Service
LF	Ledger Folio
LG	Letter of Guarantee
LIFT	Local Improvement Finance Trust
LILO	Lease In/Lease Out
LIQ	Liquid
LLC	Low Low Costs
LMV	Labour Material Voucher

LO	Local Order
LOC	Letters Of Comment
LOI	List Of Items
LOR	Letters Of Response
LP	Loan Proceed
LPD	Last Purchase Date
LPI	Late Payment Interest
LPO	Local Purchase Order
LPO	Lower Payment Option
LQA	Last Quarter Annualized
LR	Loan Repayment
LRP	Loan Repayment Programme
LTF	Long Term Financing
LTV	Liquidate, Terminate, and Vacate
LTV	Loan To Value
LVR	Loan to Valuation Ratio

M

MAAA	Member of the American Academy of Actuaries
MACC	Market Assessed Cost of Capital
MACOE	Mcomulti Agent Common Operating Environment
MACRS	Modified Accelerated Cost Recovery System

MADS	Maximum Annual Debt Service
MAF	Monthly After the Fact
MAM	Modern Accountancy Marketing
MAP	Management of an Accounting Practice
MAP	Minimum Advertised Price
MAS	Management Advisory Services
MAS	Multi Agent System
MASS	Memorandum Account Statement System
MAT	Moving Annual Total
MBA	Masters of Business Administration
MBAA	Mortgage Bankers Association of America
MBO	Management By Objective
MBS	Multi Bank Standard
MC	Marketing Cost
MC	Master Card
MC	Master Charge (now called MasterCard)
MCA	Multifamily Capital Access
MCC	Mortgage Credit Certificate
MCP	Monthly Capitation Payment
MCS	Management Consulting Services
MD	Money Deficient
MDC	Miscellaneous Debits and Credits
MDE	Minimum Distributor Earnings
MDO	Minimum Distribution Option
MEA	Major Expense Authorization
MER	Micro Economic Reform
MFOA	Municipal Finance Officers Association

MFR	Maximum Financial Return
MGM	Money Growing Money
MGR	Monthly Gross Revenue
MIA	Merchant Initiated Authorization
MIBOR	Mumbai Inter-Bank Offered Rate
MIN	Manufacturers Identification Number
MIS	Management Information System
MLB	Material, Labour, Burden
MLR	Minimum Lending Rate
MM	Material Management
MMDA	Money Market Demand Account
MMRP	Minimum Monthly Required Payment
MNA	Multi-National Account
MOH	Manufacturing Over Head
MPP	Monthly Purchase Plan
MPR	Minimum Price Required
MPS	Masterfile Payment System
MQ	Minimum Quantity
MR	Management Result
MR	Marginal Revenue
MRA	Multi Record Action
MRC	Monthly Recurring Charge
MRO	Main Refinancing Operation
MRO	Maintenance Repair and Operating
MRP	Material Requirement Planning
MRP	Maximum Retail Price
MS	Money Supply

MSBA	Michigan State Board of Accountancy
MSC	Merchant Service Charge
MSF	Manufacturing Science and Finance
MSF	Manufacturing Science Finance
MSP	Manufacturer's Selling Price
MSV	Managing for Shareholder Value
MSV	Mortgage Submission Voucher
MTD	Month To Date
MTDC	Modified Total Direct Costs
MTFP	Medium Term Fiscal Plan
MTS	Money Transactions System
MUFR	Manual for Uniform Financial Reporting
MUM	Money Under Management
MVA	Market Value Added

N

NAA	National Association of Accountants (Now IMA)
NAAACPA	National Association of Asian American Certified Public Accountants
NAAI	National Association of Accountants in Insolvencies
NAARS	National Automated Accounting Research System
NABA	National Association of Black Accountants
NACC	National Accounts Classification Committee

NAFC	National Accounting and Finance Council
NASBA	National Association of State Boards of Accountancy
NASDAQ	National Association of Securities Dealers Automated Quotations
NB	Net Benefit
NBAD	National Bank of Abu Dhabi
NBP	National Bank of Pakistan
NBR	Non Borrowed Reserves
NBT	Non Billable Time
NC	No Credit
NC	Non Collectible
NCCPAP	National Conference of Certified Public Accountant Practitioners
NCGA	National Council of Governmental Accounting
NCPAG	National Certified Public Accountant Group
NCS	Net Common Stock
NDI	Net Disposable Income
NFE	Net Foreign Earnings
NFP	Net Factor Payments
NFP	Not For Profit
NFV	Net Future Value
NFW	Net Future Worth
NIBT	Net Income Before Tax
NIFO	Next In, First Out
NIO	Not In Order
NIRS	Non-increasing Returns to Scale
NISS	National Information Services and Systems
NLR	Net License Revenue
NLR	Net Local Revenue

NM	Net Margin
NO	Normal Output
NOD	Notice Of Default
NOF	New Opportunity Funds
NOI	Net Operating Income
NOL	Net Operating Loss
NOLC	Net Operating Loss Carryover
NOPAT	Net Operating Profit After Taxes
NP	Net Profit
NPAT	Net Profit After tax
NPC	Net Present Cost
NPD	National Purchase Diary
NR	Net Revenue
NR	No Reserve
NRR	Normal Rate of Return
NRV	Non-return Valve
NS	Non-sale
NSA	Not Seasonally Adjusted
NSAA	National State Auditors' Association
NSAC	National Society of Accountants for Cooperatives
NSI	Net Sales Income
NSP	Net Selling Price
NSP	Not Separately Priced
NSV	Net Sales Value
NT	Non-transactions
NTA	Net Tangible Assets
NTF	No Transaction Fees

NUI	Net Unearned Income
NV	No Value
NVD	No Value Declared
NYB	New York Banks
NYSSCPA	New York State Society of Certified Public Accountants

O

OAC	On Approved Credit
OAR	Overhead Absorption Rate
OAS	Overpayments and Accounting Summary
OBM	Open Book Management
OBO	Or Best Offer
OCA	Open Checking Account
OCC	Other Charges and Credits
OCF	Operating Cash Flow
OCR	Official Cash Rate
OD	Overnight Deposits
OE	Open Entry
OE	Operating Expenses
OEI	Outside Equity Interest

OFR	Operating and Financial Review
OFX	Open Financial Exchange
OHD	Overhead
OI	Open Interest
OI	Operating Income
OJ	Official Journal
OLA	On-line Accounting
OLE	Old Ledger Extension
OLE	On-line Entry
OLER	On-line Entry Requirements
OLJ	On-line Journal
OMB	Office of Management and Budget
OMV	Open Market Value
ON	Order Number
OOC	Out Of Cash
OOE	Other Operating Expenses
OOPS	Outstanding Overdraft Protection Service
OPB	Outstanding Principal Balance
OPEX	OPerational EXpenditure
OPI	Open Payment Initiative
OR	Operating Result
OR	Operations Research
OS	On Sheet
OSD	Overages, Shortages, and Damages
OTB	Off Trial Balance
OTR	Order To Receipt
OTS	One Time Settlement
OTT	Over The Top
OWB	Over Without Bill

P

P	Price
P	Profit
P	Projected
P/B	Price-book Ratio
PA	Pre Approved
PA	Public Accountant
PA	Public Administration
PAB	Professional Auditor Bulletins
PAC	Pre-authorized Cheque
PACA	Per Annum Compounded Annually
PED	Pre-authorized Electronic Debit
PAF	Payment Approval Form
PAID	Production Accounting and Invoicing Database
PAL	Passive Activity Loss
PAL	Programmatic Adjustment Loan
PAN	Personal Account Number
PAP	Pre-authorized Payment
PAR	Pre-authorized Remittance
PAR	Public Accounting Report
PARIS	Purchasing, Accounting, Reporting, Information, System
PAT	Profit After Tax

PATA	Pacific Association of Tax Administrators
PB	Previous Balance
PB	Private Bank
PBB	Performance Based Budgeting
PBO	Projected Benefit Obligation
PBT	Profit Before Tax
PC	Per Capita
PCA	Priority Collection Action
PCF	Product Cost Function
PCM	Per Calculated Month
PCM	Price Cost Margin
PCM	Project Cost Model
PCS	Price Computing Scale
PCT	Primary Care Trusts
PD	Partial Deduction
PD	Probability of Default
PDD	Paperless Direct Debit
PDF	Payroll Discrepancy Form
PDI	Practice Development Institute
PDN	Payment Due Notice
PDQ	Pallet Deal Quantity
PE	Price Earnings
P/ERG	Price/Earnings Ratio to Growth
PEP	Productivity Efficiency and Profits
PERT	Performance Evaluation Reporting Technique
PFC	Prepaid Finance Charge
PFP	Personal Financial Planning

PFS	Personal Financial Specialist
PI	Pre-invoice
PIE	Price Implied Expectations
PIF	Payment In Full
PIK	Payment In Kind
PIL	Payment In Lieu
PIL	Percentage Increase in Loss
PILOT	Payment In Lieu Of Taxes
PIP	Penalty Interest Payments
PIP	Price Interest Percentage
PIP	Purchasing Invoice Problem
PIT	Principal Interest and Taxes
PITI	Principal Interest Tax and Insurance
PL	Plan Loan
PLL	Provision for Loan Loss
PLS	Profit and Loss Sharing
PLU	Price Look Up
PMI	Preferred Minimum Interest
PML	Probable Maximum Loss
PMS	Payment Management System
PMV	Presumed Maximum Value
PO	Production Order
PO	Purchase Order
POB	Public Oversight Board
POD	Payable On Demand
POI	Price and Output Indices
POP	Point Of Purchase

POR	Pay On Return
POR	Payable On Receipt
POR	Price On Request
POS	Percentage Of Sales
POS	Purchase Of Service
PP	Pre Paid
PPS	Payment Processing Service
PPS	Prospective Payment System
PPV	Price Per Variance
PPV	Purchase Price Variance
PR	Price Received
PR	Programme Revenue
PRC	Peer Review Committee
PRD	Price Related Differential
PRS	Payment Reminder System
PRSA	Pension Retirement Savings Accounts
PS	Point Source
PS	Purchase Sale
PSA	Personal Savings Account
PSFI	Private Sector Financed Infrastructure
PSNB	Public Sector Net Borrowing
PTI	Pre-tax Income
PTIN	Preparer Tax Identification Number
PTN	Product Transfer Notes
PTO	Payment Treatment and Operations
PTP	Pre-tax Profit
PTP	Publicly Traded Partnership

PTP	Purchase To Pay
PTPD	Part Paid
PTPM	Pre-tax Profit Margin
PTPP	Pre-tax Premium Plan
PV	Present Value
PV	Principle Value
PVA	Present Value Analysis
PVCHART	Profit-Volume Chart
PVIF	Present Value Interest Factor
PVIFA	Present Value Interest Factor for Annuities

Q

QAB	Quarterly Account Balance
QAI	Quality Auditing Institute
QC	Quality Control
QC	Quantity Comparison
QCIC	Quality Control Inquiry Committee
QCP	Quality Control Policies and Procedures
QCR	Qualifying Collateral Report
QDA	Quantity Discount Agreement

QO	Quote Order
QOF	Quality Of Finance
QOH	Quantity On Hand
QP	Quantity Purchased
QR	Quality Review Programme
QTD	Quarter To Date
QTD	Quoted
QTIP	Qualified Terminable Interest Property
QTIP	Qualified Terminal Interest Property
QTQ	Quarter To Quarter
QTR	Quarter

R

R	Rate
R	Revenue
RA	Remuneration and Audit
RA	Return Authorization
RAL	Rapid Anticipation Loan
RAL	Refund Anticipation Loan
RAPS	Reimbursement Account Processing System
RB	Revenue Book
RBC	Risk Based Capital

RC	Rate Change
RC	Reduced Cost
RCTI	Recipient Created Tax Invoice
REAL	Revenues Expenses Assets Liabilities
REIT	Real Estate Investment Trust
REV	Revenue
REW	Real Estate Withholding
RFA	Recency Frequency and Amount
RFP	Request For Proposal
RFV	Relative Fair Value
RGP	Redemption Grace Period
RI	Real Interest
RI	Residual Income
RIA	Residual Intangible Assets
RIF	Registered Investment Plan
RITC	Reduced Income Tax Credit
RLF	Revolving Loan Fund
RM	Retail Margin
RMB	Reimburse
RMD	Required Minimum Distribution
RMM	Retirement Money Management
RMS	Receivables Management Service
RMS	Receivables Management Solutions
RMU	Reticular Module Unit
RNY	Required Net Yield
ROA	Return On Average
ROC	Retail Only Consumer

ROC	Return On Capital
ROC	Running On Credit
ROD	Return On Debt
ROE	Rate Of Exchange
ROE	Return On Equity
ROEC	Return On Economic Capital
ROG	Rate Of Growth
ROIA	Research Opportunities in Internal Auditing
ROIA	Return On Investment Analysis
ROIC	Return On Invested Capital
ROII	Return On Inventory Investment
ROIT	Return On Investment from Technology
ROIV	Return On Investment Value
ROIM	Return On Investment Multiple
ROMI	Return On Market Investment
ROP	Reciprocity Of Price
ROR	Rate Of Return
ROSS	Resource Ordering and Status System
RP	Regular Price
RP	Risk Premium
RPD	Revenue Processing Division
RPH	Rate Per Hour
RPO	Rapid Purchase Order
RPPS	Remote Payment and Presentment Service
RPS	Remittance Processing Service
RR	Receiving Record
RRA	Revenue Reconciliation Act of 1990

RRB	Real Return Bonds
RRB	Resource Related Billing
RRDA	Repetitive Record Distribution Audit
RRI	Risk Return Index
RRM	Realty Rate Monitor
RRR	Required Reserve Ratio
RSPA	Research Sponsored Programmes Accounting
RT	Routing and Transit number
RTD	Revenue Transmittal Document
RTGS	Real Time Gross Settlement
RTPP	Real Time Payments Processing
RTPS	Real Time Payment System
RTV	Return To Vendor
RV	Revaluation

S

SAAR	Seasonally Adjusted Annualized Rate
SAARS	Standard Accounting And Review Standards
SAB	Staff Accounting Bulletins
SAC	Same As Cash
SACS	Standardized Account Code Structure
SAFE	Secure Automated Financial Exchange
SAFR	Standard Accounting For Retail
SAICA	South African Institute of Chartered Accountants
SAL	Structural Adjustment Loan
SALY	Same As Last Year
SAP	Service Advertisement Protocol
SAP	Standard Accounting Procedures
SAP	Systems Applications Products
SAPG	Sector Accounting Policies Group
SAR	Salvation And Revival
SAS	Semi Annual Statement
SAS	Statistical Analysis System
SBA	Small Business Administration
SBPOA	Shared Services and Business Process Outsourcing Association
SBT	Scan Based Trading
SCON	Scheme Contracted Out Number
SCR	Stranded Costs Recovered

SCRR	Special Cash Reserve Requirement
SDB	Safe Deposit Box
SDU	State Disbursement Unit
SDX	Secure Document exchange
SEC	Securities and Exchange Commission
SECPS	Securities and Exchange Commission Practice Section
SEDA	Standby Equity Distribution Agreement
SEPP	Simplified Employee Pension Plan
SERP	Supplemental Employee Retirement Plan
SET	Secure Electronic Transaction
SF	Structural Funds
SF	Surcharge Free
SFAC	Statements of Fiscal Accounting Concepts
SFAS	Statement of Financial Accounting Standards
SFE	Sales Force Effectiveness
SFS	Shared Financial System
SGA	Sales General and Administrative
SGA	Selling, General, and Administrative
SGL	Subsidiary General Ledger
SGM	Standard Gross Margin
SIA	Society of Insurance Accountants
SIAS	Statements on Internal Auditing Standards
SIP	Sales Inventory Purchase
SIR	Statistical Inventory Reconciliation
SKR	Safekeeping Receipts
SLAM	Super Low Administrative Mortgage
SLC	Sight Letter of Credit

SLR	Statutory Liquidity Ratio
SMA	Separately Managed Account
SMA	Special Memorandum Account
SMART	Systematic Mortgage Amortization Reduction Technology
SMAS	Statements of Standards for Management Advisory Services
SNBG	State Network on Block Grants
SNC	Shared National Credits
SOA	Statement Of Activity
SODA	Standing Order Deposit Account
SOE	Start Of Entry
SOFA	Statement Of Financial Activities
SOHO	Small Office/ Home Office
SOI	Schedule Of Investment
SOP	Sale Of Purchase
SOP	Statements Of Position
SOS	Start Out Savings
SPAN	School Property Account Number
SPAR	Special Pricing Agreements And Rebates
SPD	State Price Density
SPF	Sale Pending Funds
SPFV	Series Payment Future Value
SPI	Store Payment Interface
SPN	Secure Payment Network
SPOF	Supply Price Of Finance
SPOT	Secure Payment for Online Transactions
SPP	Simple Payback Period
SPQR	Small Profit Quick Return

SPRV	Special Purpose Re-insurance Vehicle
SQ	Standard Quantity
SRAC	Short Run Average Cost
SRLY	Separate Return Limitation Year
SRM	Summary Review Memorandum
SRMC	Short Run Marginal Cost
SRPI	Self Report and Projective Inventory
SS	Sum of Sales
SSA	Special Savings Account
SSAE	Statements on Standards for Attestation Engagements
SSAP	Statement of Statutory Accounting Principal
SSARS	SS Accounting and Review Services
SSARI	SS Accounting and Review Interpretations
SSASPFI	SS Accountants' Services on Prospective Financial Information
SSN	Sales Sequenced Number
ST	Sub Total
STBF	Subject To Booking Fee
STBP	Short Term Business Payment
STI	Short Term Incentive
STL	Short Term Loan
STRIP	Separately Traded Residual and Interest Payments
SUQ	Standard Update Quantity
SUTA	State Unemployment Tax Act
SV	Sales Volume
SYD	Sum-of-the-years'- Digits

T

T	Total
T/T	Telegraphic Transfer
TAA	Trade Adjustment Assistance
TAB	Tax Anticipation Bill
TABS	Telephone Account Billing System
TAC	Targeted Amortization Class
TAC	Total Average Cost
TAF	Term Auction Facility
TAMRA	Technical and Miscellaneous Revenue Act of 1998
TAS	The Accounting Solution
TBL	Triple Bottom Line
TBO	Total Bookkeeping Operations
TBR	Total Business Return
TC	Total Cost
TCAN	Tax Credit Award Notice
TCE	Tax Counseling of the Elderly
TCO	Take Cost Out
TCO	Total Cost of Ownership
TD	Tabular Data
TDR	Total Debt Restructuring
TDS	Tax Deduction at Source
TDS	Total Debt Service

TE	Total Expenditure
TE	Total Expenses
TEC	Total Employment Cost
TEC	Total End Cost
TEFRA	Tax Equity and Fiscal Responsibility Act of 1982
TEL	Tax Expenditure Limitation
TFM	Total Financial Management
TFSA	Tax-free Savings Account
TGR	Total Gross Receipts
TI	Transcribe In
TIC	Technical Issues Committee
TIC	Total Input Costs
TIC	True Interest Cost
TIF	Tax Increment Financing
TIFA	Tax Increment Financing Authority
TIGER	Technology Industry And Government for E-Revolution
TIS	Transaction Information System
TITCP	Technology Investment Tax Credit Program
TJ	Transposed Journals
TLC	Too Little Cash
TLC	Too Little Credit
TMA	Tax on Management Account
TMP	Tax Matters Partner
TNW	Total Net Worth
TOA	Total Operating Assets
TOD	Transfer On Death
TP	Transfer Pricing

TPR	Total Price Reduction
TPT	Tax on Prior Transfers
TR	Total Revenue
TR	Trust Receipt
TRAC	Transactional Records Access Clearinghouse
TRC	Total Resource Cost
TRX	Transaction
TS	Total Surplus
TSC	Transaction Service Charge
TSC	True Stranded Costs
TSTE	Two Stage Transaction Execution
TTM	Trailing Twelve Months
TTP	Time To Pay
TV	Transfer Voucher
TVC	Total Variable Costs
TVM	Time Value of Money
TVT	Time Value Tangibles
TXN	Transaction
TXP	Tax Payment
TXR	Tax Supplemental Return

U

UCC	Unconfirmed Credit Contract
UCC	Uniform Commercial Code
UCR	Un-cassified Receipts
UCR	Usable Capital Receipts
UDI	User Defined Invoicing
UEC	Union Europeene des Experts Comptables Economiques et Financiers
UNI	Undistributed Net Income
UOI	Unit Of Inquiry
UPB	Unamortized Principle Balance
UPIC	Universal Payment Identification Code
UPL	Upper Payment Limit
UPRICE	Unit Price
URN	Unique Reference Number
USFV	Uniform Series Future Value
USPV	Uniform Series Present Value
USTC	United States Tax Court
UTA	Under Trust Agreement
UTD	Up To Date
UVX	Universal Value exchange

V

VAA	Value Added Auditing
VAN	Value Added Note
VAP	Visa Authenticated Payments
VBV	Verified By Visa
VC	Variable Costs
VCF	Venture Capital Financing
VCM	Variable Contribution Margin
VCT	Volatile Capital Tax
VFM	Value For Money
VIF	Variance Inflation Factor
VJI	View Journal Invoice
VLI	Very Low Inflation
VMP	Value of Marginal Product
VMS	Voucher Management System
VOD	Verification Of Deposit
VOM	Value Of Money
VPF	Vice President, Finance
VRM	Variable Rate Mortgage
VSDC	Visa Smart Debit Card
VSP	Very Secure Payment
VTS	Virtual Transaction Systems

W

WAA	Washington Association of Accountants
WAC	With Approved Credit
WACC	Weighted Average Cost of Capital
WACC	Weighted Average Costs of Capital
WACR	Weighted Average Certificate Rate
WADR	Weighted Average Deposit Rate
WAV	With Added Value
WBLS	Web-based Loan Summary Sheet
WCAH	World Congress of Accounting Historians
WCAR	Western Canadian Auditing Roundtable
WCFG	Working Capital For Growth
WCFI	World Class Financial Infrastructure
WCFN	Working Capital Financing Needs
WCFO	Working Capital Fund Operations
WCV	Weighted Collateral Value
WDDA	Wholesale Demand Deposit Account
WDV	Written Down Value
WFFP	Web Funds Financial Processing
WGA	Whole of Government Accounts
WI	With Interest
WI	Working Investment

WIN	Work Incentive Credit
WMER	Wholesale Management And Efficiency Report
WNQ	Will Not Quote
WO	Write Off
WRCC	Western Region Credit Conference
WRIS	Wage Record Interchange System
WSP	Wholesale Price
WSQ	Will Send Quote
WSV	Wholesale Sales Volume
WSV	Wholesale Value
WUAA	Washington University Accounting Association
WUMT	Western Union Money Transfer

X

XH	Extra High
XP	Extra Profit
XTF	Xpress Tax Forms

Y

YC	Year Corrected
YLD	Yield
YOY	Year On Year
YTY	Year to Year

Z

ZB	Zero Balance
ZBA	Zero Balance Account
ZBB	Zero Base Budget
ZIRP	Zero Interest Rate Policy
ZQ	Zero Quantity

End

7 Interview Tips

Resume Writing Tips

Resume should be well written to increase the chance of being invited for an interview. The candidate should take effort to create a resume that will make him stand among other probable candidates, so resume is the professional reflection of individuals who are applying or looking for a job or employment. When candidates are writing a resume arrange all the necessary documents, certificates and gather all the important information need for writing the resume. Recall all your career plans for a good resume format. Regardless of the format, all resume contain the same information that should be presented and stated very well to yield positive results. Apply for those jobs and positions that would fit on qualifications and personality. The candidate must first understand what the company is looking for and identify the candidate have that significant qualifications for the particular position or job wish to apply.

Your objective should be based on your career plan and should likewise concede with what the company needs. Establish your objective in such a way that you can convey to the employer that you are just the right candidate they're looking for. Mention the exact position you are applying on the Objective Section to demonstrate clarity. Suppose the candidate have the experience, candidate should begin with job titles, followed by the company name or *vice versa*, depending which is more remarkable and must stick to it for consistency. Include all work-related experience under this section including the internships and voluntary works and services. Better to list experience in reverse chronological order and write the dates after each work have done excluding the months unless the job is held for less than a year.

Once finished work experience section the candidate mention educational qualification. State the major course and awards but don't include other small commendations. After education section the candidate can write some of personal background or interest. Personal interest, when properly listed demonstrates the candidate's versatility. But always write that are somehow relevant on the company or the position being applied.

Reference section is the final section of the resume. Prepare them in another sheet and present only when being asked by the employer. The candidate can mention as "Reference available upon request" under the reference section. So with these useful tips start writing resume and apply for the job you are searching.

Top Job Interview Questions

A list of the top 10 job interview questions, before attending for an interview many interview questions are to be expected and prepared before attending for an interview. Study this list of interview questions and plan your answers ahead of time so you'll be ready to deliver them with confidence.

1. Can you tell us why are you choosing this company? And why do you want to work for us?
2. Can you explain a situation where you didn't meet your goals or objectives?
3. Explain a situation where you faced conflict or difficult communication problems?
4. If your current manager has to tell about your strengths and weeknesses what would be your strengths and weeknesses?
5. Where do you see yourself in 1/3/5 years time?
6. Can you justify yourself why should we give you this job?
7. Tell us a situation you have faced with a huge challenge or worked to an unreasonable deadline?
8. Do you prefer working your own or in a team?
9. If you were to start working with our company what is the first thing you would change?
10. Have you ever had a conflict with a boss/colleague/professor or with your family members? How was it resolved?

Tips to Take Control of Our Life

Taking control of our life is getting in touch with our values, identifying our vision and setting meaningful goals. To understand where our life is taking and to have control of ourself means being more productive, dealing more effectively with stress, having the ability to solve problems, accepting change and developing healthy optimism. Practice certain steps and we are on our way to success.

1. Get in touch with values:
2. What is important to me?
3. What do I need to do to feel good about myself?
4. Who is important to me?
5. What or who is most important? Be honest with yourself.
6. How would you feel if someone you respect knew this was one of your values?
7. Would you stick by this value?
8. How is this value affecting your life?

Job Interview Questions About You

- What is your greatest weakness?
- What is your greatest strength?
- Describe a typical work week.
- Do you take work home with you?
- How many hours do you normally work?
- How would you describe the pace at which you work?
- How do you handle stress and pressure?
- What motivates you?
- What are your salary expectations?
- What do you find are the most difficult decisions to make?
- Tell me about yourself.
- What has been the greatest disappointment in your life?
- What are you passionate about?
- What are your pet peeves?

Common Interview Questions and Answers:

Tell me About Yourself:

The most often asked question in interviews. You need to have a short statement prepared in your mind. Be careful that it does not sound rehearsed. Talk about things you have done and jobs you have held that relate to the position you are interviewing for.

Why did you leave your last job?

Stay positive regardless of the circumstances. Never refer to a major problem with management and never speak ill of supervisors, co-workers or the organization. If you do, you will be the one looking bad. Keep smiling and talk about leaving for a positive reason such as an opportunity, a chance to do something special or other forward-looking reasons.

What experience do you have in this field?

Speak about specifics that relate to the position you are applying for. If you do not have specific experience, get as close as you can.

What do you know about this organization?

This question is one reason to do some research on the organization before the interview. Find out where they have been and where they are going. What are the current issues and who are the major players?

What have you done to improve your knowledge in the last year?

Try to include improvement activities that relate to the job. A wide variety of activities can be mentioned as positive self-improvement. Have some good ones handy to mention.

Are you applying for other jobs?

Be honest but do not spend a lot of time in this area. Keep the focus on this job and what you can do for this organization.

Why do you want to work for this organization?

This may take some thought and certainly, should be based on the research you have done on the organization. Sincerity is extremely important here and will easily be sensed. Relate it to your long-term career goals.

What kind of salary do you need?

A nasty little game that you will probably lose if you answer first. So, do not answer it. In most cases, the interviewer, taken off guard, will tell you. If not, say that it can depend on the details of the job.

Are you a team player?

Of course, a team player. Be sure to have examples ready. Specifics that show you often perform for the good of the team rather than for yourself are good evidence of your team attitude. Do not brag; just say it in a matter-of-fact tone. This is a key point.

How long would you expect to work for us if hired?

Specifics here are not good. Something like this should work: I'd like it to be a long time. Or As long as we both feel I'm doing a good job.

Have you ever been asked to leave a position?

If you have not, say no. If you have, be honest, brief and avoid saying negative things about the people or organization involved.

Explain how you would be an asset to this organization.

You should be anxious for this question. It gives you a chance to highlight your best points as they relate to the position being discussed. Give a little advance thought to this relationship.

Why should we hire you?

Point out how your assets meet what the organization needs. Do not mention any other candidates to make a comparison.

What is your greatest strength?

Numerous answers are good, just stay positive. A few good examples: Your ability to prioritize, your problem-solving skills, your ability to work under pressure, your ability to focus on projects, your professional expertise, your leadership skills, your positive attitude.

Why do you think you would do well at this job?

Give several reasons and include skills, experience and interest.

What is more important to you: the money or the work?

Money is always important, but the work is the most important. There is no better answer.

Tell me about your ability to work under pressure.

You may say that you thrive under certain types of pressure. Give an example that relates to the type of position applied for.

What motivates you to do your best on the job?

This is a personal trait that only you can say, but good examples are: Challenge, Achievement, Recognition.

Are you willing to work overtime? Nights? Weekends?

This is up to you. Be totally honest.

Would you be willing to relocate if required?

You should be clear on this with your family prior to the interview if you think there is a chance it may come up. Do not say yes just to get the job if the real answer is no. This can create a lot of problems later on in your career. Be honest at this point.

If you were hiring a person for this job, what would you look for?

Be careful to mention traits that are needed and that you have.

What qualities do you look for in a boss?

Be generic and positive. Safe qualities are knowledgeable, a sense of humour, fair, loyal to subordinates and holder of high standards. All bosses think they have these traits.

Describe your work ethic.

Emphasize benefits to the organization. Things like, determination to get the job done and work hard but enjoy your work are good.

Tell me about the most fun you have had on the job.

Talk about having fun by accomplishing something for the organization.

Do you have any questions for me?

Always have some questions prepared. Questions prepared where you will be an asset to the organization are good. How soon will I be able to be productive? and what type of projects will I be able to assist on? There are the.

Campus Interview Preparation Tips

A number of companies visit campus each semester to interview seniors for professional entry-level positions that start after graduation and current students for career related internships. Are you getting ready to leave your college and you are anxiously getting ready for your job search. Campus interviews can be nerve-wrecking for any student.